Y0-ELA-587

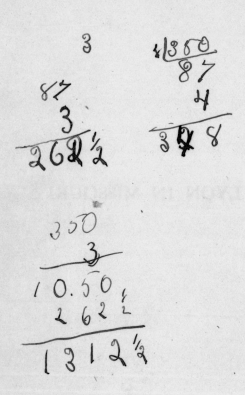

```
        3              4)350
      87                 87
       3                  4
    ─────────         ─────────
    262½              3 7 8

        350
          3
       ─────────
      10.50
       262½
    ─────────────
      1312½
```

WITH LYON IN MISSOURI

THE YOUNG KENTUCKIANS SERIES

By BYRON A. DUNN

GENERAL NELSON'S SCOUT
ON GENERAL THOMAS'S STAFF
BATTLING FOR ATLANTA
FROM ATLANTA TO THE SEA
RAIDING WITH MORGAN

Illustrated, 12mo, per volume, $1.25

A. C. McClurg & Co., Publishers
CHICAGO

"Oh! you will save me, won't you?"

[*Page 249*]

WITH
LYON IN MISSOURI

BY

BYRON A. DUNN

Author of "General Nelson's Scout," etc.

WITH EIGHT ILLUSTRATIONS
BY H. S. DeLAY

CHICAGO
A. C. McCLURG & CO.
1910

COPYRIGHT
A. C. McCLURG & CO.
1910

Published September 24, 1910

All Rights Reserved.

The Lakeside Press
R. R. DONNELLEY & SONS COMPANY
CHICAGO

LYON

True to his convictions; true to his flag; true to the Union men of Missouri who confided in and followed him; true to himself, and true to duty, he went out to battle against a force twice as great as his own, with a calmness that was as pathetic as his courage was sublime.

—Colonel Thomas L. Snead.

PREFACE

IT is some years since the author gave to the public the "Young Kentuckians Series" of tales of the Civil War; and this volume he now launches upon the sea of literature, hoping that it may receive as gracious a reception from the youths of the country as did "General Nelson's Scout."

As that book dealt with the struggle to hold Kentucky in the Union, so this deals with the struggle which held Missouri. The contest for Missouri was ten-fold more intense than that for Kentucky, for in it the Federal authorities had to meet the hostility of the entire State Government, composed of brave and determined men.

For the historical facts, he has examined the Official Records, and many books and articles which bear on the subject; also he has gleaned many things from his personal acquaintance with those who were actors in the scenes. But to no book has he been so much indebted as to Colonel Thomas L. Snead's "The Fight for Missouri." Colonel Snead is a singularly frank and honest writer. He was in a position where he was cognizant of the secret movements of the State Government in its efforts to take the State out of the Union, and these he has revealed. He was a brave, gallant, and honest foe.

In General Nathaniel Lyon this book deals with one of the grandest and noblest characters of the war, a character too little known to the rising generation. The mighty events which followed his death have obscured, and in a measure caused to be forgotten, what he did. No man in so short a time accomplished so much. A grateful nation should erect a monument to his memory, and on that monument should be inscribed the tribute paid to him by one who fought against him, and to whom this book is dedicated.

BYRON A. DUNN.

WAUKEGAN, ILL., *August, 1910*.

CONTENTS

ILLUSTRATIONS

WITH LYON IN MISSOURI

CHAPTER I

THE MOB

THE Platte of Missouri is a small river which
runs through the northwest portion of the
State, and empties into the Missouri River
a little above Leavenworth, Kansas. Early in the
month of October, 1856, a strange scene was being
enacted on the banks of this stream, a few miles
above Platte City. An infuriated mob had gathered, and in the midst of the mob was a shivering,
terrified man, stripped to the skin. Near by a kettle
of tar was being warmed over a small fire; and one
of the mob was ripping open a feather pillow with
an ugly-looking knife.

Near the stripped, shivering man stood a little
boy, not more than eleven or twelve years of age,
wringing his hands, and with the tears streaming
down his cheeks, crying, "Please don't kill papa!
Please don't kill papa!"

"Shut up, you imp of Satan, or we'uns will give
you the same dose we'uns are goin' to give your il-
lustrous dad," growled one of the mob as he caught
the boy by the collar, and roughly threw him back.

1

The boy fell heavily and for a moment lay stunned, then he slowly struggled to his feet; but he was no longer crying. Instead, his little fists were clinched, and his eyes were blazing. "Cowards! Cowards!" he cried. "Oh, that I were a man!"

"An' what would you do, if you was a man?" asked his tormentor, chuckling.

"Fight you, fight the whole of you! You are a pack of cowards!" cried the boy boldly.

The man scowled, started toward the boy, as if to crush him, but changed his mind, and satisfied himself by saying: "Look heah, my little bantam, you crow loud, but it would be bettah for you and yo' pa both, if you kept a civil tongue in yo' head. As it is, I have a mind to wring yo' neck, you abolition brat."

"Never mind the boy now, Jake," spoke up one of the mob who seemed to be the leader; "the tar is warm enough, and when we get through with this nigger-stealing abolition preacher his own son won't know him. It will be a fine lesson for the boy, not to tread in the footsteps of his dad."

"All right," growled the other, "but the brat has got to keep his mouth shut, or I will wring his neck. Jake Dempsey is n't used to bein' called a coward."

The victim, who was a minister of the gospel, now spoke for the first time. "Lawrence, you can do me no good," he said gently to his son. "Do not say anything to bring the anger of these men against you." Then looking into the scowling faces of the mob, the minister continued: "Surely you will spare my child. He has done no harm. You are not all demons. No doubt some of you have children of your own. Think of them, and spare my boy. As for me, I am in the hands of the Lord. As my Master bore the buffeting of the mob with meekness, so will I try to bear whatever indignities you may heap upon me."

"Ha! ha!" laughed the leader, "that is a good one. A North Methodist preacher in the hands of the Lord! You had better pray to your master, the Devil, if you want help. As for the Lord, we are his humble instruments to show you this is not a healthy country in which to preach abolition doctrine." Then standing before the preacher and swinging his brush before his eyes, he continued: "You should have heard Elder Perkins last Sunday. He preached a beautiful sermon, showing how according to the Scriptures it was right to hold the nigger in bondage; so you are not only breaking the laws of Missouri, but you are going against the Bible. What have you got to say for yourself?"

The preacher's lips moved as if in prayer, but he did not answer.

"Nothing to say, eh? Well, this court will at once proceed to business. I am going to give you the dandiest dress suit you ever wore, one you will be proud of."

Thus saying, he dipped the brush into the warm tar, and amid the jeers and laughter of the mob who crowded around, he brought it with a sweep, across the preacher's breast.

"Black abolitionist he is, and black we will make him," he exclaimed.

For a moment the boy stood transfixed with horror, then before the man had time to apply the tar again, with a cry which sounded more like the angry snarl of a wild beast than human, he sprang forward, and fastened his teeth into the wrist of the leader; and he had to be shaken off like a dog before he would let go. With a fearful oath, the leader seized the boy, and walking to the river threw him far out into the stream. The father gave one cry of agony, then breaking from his captors, he sprang forward to rescue his son. The leader caught him just as he was about to plunge into the river. He struggled like a maniac, and more than one of the mob bore marks of his blows, his nails and teeth.

His struggles had called attention away from Lawrence, and after the minister had been thoroughly subdued, one of the mob went to look after the boy, but he was nowhere to be seen.

"Reckon he is food for the catfish, all right," coolly remarked the fellow as he walked back.

"Oh! my poor boy! My poor boy!" wailed the minister, "would God I had died for you!"

He had been roughly handled in his struggles, but he did not seem to mind his bruises. He thought only of his son, now, as he supposed, lying in the slimy bed of the river. The leader looked at his wrist ruefully. It was badly torn, and blood was dripping from his hand.

"Better put some of the tar on it, Bill, it will stop the bleeding," said one of the men. "There will be enough left for the preacher."

Ketcham, for that was the leader's name, did as was suggested, and then binding his handkerchief around the injured member, was ready to proceed. "I will just give you double the dose that I intended, on account of this wrist," he growled.

He then proceeded to smear the minister with the tar from head to feet, leaving only the face untouched. "I would cover that, too," he remarked, "but it would shut off his wind; and I want him to live, so he can see what a beautiful object he is!"

The feathers were then applied, a large tuft being placed on the top of his head. As the mob looked on the object they had created, they danced and yelled with delight. The Reverend Arthur Middleton was certainly a grotesque-looking object.

"Beautiful! beautiful!" exclaimed Ketcham as he walked around and surveyed his job. "Boys, he ought to have his picture taken."

Then taking off his hat, he said, "This glorious gathering ought not to break up without a suitable toast in honor of him who has furnished the entertainment. Here is to the preacher! May his dress become the fashion for every one who follows in his footsteps!"

"Hold on! We must drink to that toast," cried one, and he pulled a bottle of whiskey out of his pocket. The toast was drunk amid the greatest enthusiasm.

The sun was now low in the west, and the question arose what disposition they should make of their victim. "Let's hang him, now, as a scarecrow," said one, as he nursed a swollen nose, that Mr. Middleton had given him in his struggles.

"No," said another, "that would be too merciful. Let's leave him to wander where he will; the poor devil will soon die of hunger and exposure, for even the niggers will take him for the Evil One, and flee from him."

"Why not send him to look after his precious son?" said another.

The idea instantly found favor. "Just the thing! just the thing!" they all cried.

"Say, he will be the strangest-looking animal ever seen navigating the Platte," remarked Ketcham.

A log was procured, as a means of conveyance. "Better tie him on, or the poor cuss will roll off and drown," said one more tender-hearted than the others.

"No danger; he would swim like a duck, his feathers would hold him up," remarked Ketcham, with a grin. "But tie him on, and the next we hear of him, he will be navigating the Big Muddy."

"Let me tie him on," said he of the swollen nose, "I have a grudge agin' him."

"All right, go ahead," said Ketcham.

Not only were Mr. Middleton's ankles bound beneath the log, but his hands were tied behind him.

"That is cruel," remarked one. "He does n't stand a ghost of a show now."

"What 's the use of sending him off with his hands untied," snapped Swollen Nose, "he would get himself free in no time." And he was allowed to have his way.

During the preparations, Mr. Middleton made no protest. In fact, he seemed in a daze, and not to realize what was being done to him. At last the job was done to the satisfaction of all, and the log was pushed out into the stream. The current caught it, and the mob watched it as it floated away with its human freight, until it was hid from view by a bend in the river.

"*Bon voyage*," they shouted, and with jest and banter they mounted their horses and rode swiftly away, and the shadows of night swallowed them up.

As for Mr. Middleton, the laving of his limbs by the stream somewhat revived him, but he felt faint and dizzy, and there seemed to be something gripping at his heart. He believed that death was near, but to him death had no terrors. He only prayed that it might come surely and swiftly. He grew fainter and weaker. Strange visions danced before his eyes. A lethargy stole over him, and he slowly sank forward until his head rested on the log, and now and then the water would lap his parched lips. He felt no pain, now. To him, it seemed he was floating down — down into eternity, and he murmured, "Father, receive my spirit!"

After a time the log was caught in an eddy, and drifted close to the bank, resting there, but he did not notice the fact. It was so delicious to die — to be borne along on unseen wings. The lapping of the water, the whispering of the breeze were to his ears as the far-off music of the heavenly host.

"Father!"

It was a whisper as soft as a summer zephyr. He did not notice it.

"Father!"

The whisper was louder, and it reached his dull ears. Was he already dead, and was the spirit of his son calling to him?

"Father, oh, father!"

The call was now in a low voice. It thrilled him through and through; it aroused his dormant senses.

He opened his eyes; darkness was around, but surely he had heard the voice of his son.

"Father, oh, father, do you not hear me? Can you not answer me?"

The agonized voice fully aroused him. With a great effort he sat up. The thick darkness concealed everything. But surely he had heard a voice — a voice so like his son's, that he asked faintly, "Who calls?"

"I — Lawrence. I am here to help you, father!"

"Then you were not drowned — you escaped? I am not dead, neither is this a dream, is it?" asked the bewildered man.

"No, father, you are neither dead nor dreaming. I am here, all right."

"My son alive! Father in heaven, I thank thee," exclaimed Mr. Middleton fervently.

"Now, father," said Lawrence cheerfully, "keep up good courage! I will soon have you free."

"You will find it no easy task," replied Mr. Middleton, "I am bound hands and feet."

"I know it, father, I saw it all; but I will find a way to free you," answered the brave boy.

Lawrence carefully worked his way down to the edge of the river. The bank was steep, and it was very dark, so he had to feel his way carefully, clinging to the bushes for support. He found that one end of the log on which his father was bound rested on the bank, but the other end was out in the stream. He pondered for a while, what to do, then with his pocket-knife, which fortunately had not been taken from him, he cut a stout branch of an overhanging bush, leaving a prong at the larger end. This he managed to hook over the log behind his father. It was now an easy matter to swing the log around, until its whole length rested against the bank. Clinging to the branches of the bush, he reached out and cut the cords which bound his father's wrists.

"Now, father," he said, "hold onto the bush, and I will try to find the cords which bind your ankles."

But so cold and bloodless were Mr. Middleton's hands, that it was some time before he could get any feeling or strength in them. At last he said, "I think I can hold on now, Lawrence."

To cut the cords which bound his father's limbs, Lawrence found no easy task. He had to reach far down into the water, and once he slipped into the river, nearly losing his precious knife. But at last the cords were cut, and Mr. Middleton was free.

"Now, father, try to drag yourself upon the bank, by the branch of which you have hold," said Lawrence.

By exerting all his strength, and with the aid of the boy, Mr. Middleton managed to drag himself out of the water, and to crawl slowly up the bank. When he reached the top, he lay for some time, utterly exhausted. When he could speak, he said: "How did it come you were not drowned, when they threw you into the river? I did not know you could swim."

"I can swim only a little," Lawrence answered, "but I managed to keep myself afloat; the current bore me swiftly down, and fortunately carried me near enough to the opposite bank, so I could grasp the overhanging branch of a tree. To draw myself up among the bushes and conceal myself was the work of a moment. But the mob did not seem to notice me, I think they were busy with you."

"Yes," replied Mr. Middleton, "I thought you would drown, and I broke from the mob, thinking to save you; but I was caught, and borne struggling back. I think I was insane for the moment, over the thought that you were drowning, and I fought like a madman; but what could I do against so many? But go on, my boy, what next?"

"I was completely hidden where I was," continued Lawrence, "and could watch every movement of the mob. And, oh, father! when I saw them smearing you with the tar, I could n't look. I buried my face in the leaves. I groaned, I cried, and, father," this faintly, "I swore; I cursed them. There was murder in my heart. I beat the ground with my hands; I could have torn every one of that mob limb from limb, if I had had the power."

"My son, my son, 'Vengeance is mine,' saith the

Lord; you should curse no one," answered his father.

"Why did n't the Lord strike them dead, then?" exclaimed Lawrence bitterly. "Why does not the Lord protect those who believe in Him? To my mind, He is a poor sort of a Lord to let those suffer who love Him."

The father groaned. "Lawrence, Lawrence," he wailed, "don't talk so! Don't add to my suffering. But go on, tell me the rest."

"There is not much more to tell. The mob grew strangely still, and when I looked again they were tying you to the log; and when they set you adrift, a great hope sprang up in my heart. I would follow you and free you. At first I followed cautiously, but then it grew dark, and I had no fear of being seen. My only fear was that I might lose you in the darkness, for in many places the trees and bushes shut out all view of the river. At last, as the darkness thickened, all I could see was a white spot on the water." And Lawrence shuddered as he remembered what caused that white spot.

Controlling himself, he resumed. "After a time the spot remained stationary, and I knew the log had caught; and you know the rest. Now I have you, father, all will be well. We will reach Kansas yet."

The joy of finding that his son was alive, and his own rescue from his perilous condition, had given Mr. Middleton unnatural strength, but now the reaction came. To Lawrence's hopeful words, he could only reply with a groan. Here he was naked, shivering with cold, and an object of horror to look upon. He shuddered as he touched himself; the chill of the night was striking to his very bones; and where could he go? No where in that inhospitable region. His pitiable condition overcame him, and for the first time he wept bitterly. Better had he been murdered outright.

His father's sobs nearly broke Lawrence's heart. "Don't, father, don't!" he pleaded. "Surely there is some way out of this."

"Alas! my boy," said Mr. Middleton in a quivering voice, "for me there is no help, but there may be for you. Surely they are not all savages here. There must be some kind hearts who will not drive a defenceless child from their door. Leave me, my son, and seek shelter; but, first, kiss me, and let me bless you before you go."

"What! go away and leave you?" asked Lawrence in astonishment.

"Yes, my son, it is the only way. It is better that you should live than that both should perish. Look at my condition, — naked, covered with horrible stuff, no money — "

"But, father, you forget," broke in Lawrence. "Don't you remember that but yesterday you sewed two hundred dollars in my clothes, saying that it would be safer with me than with you?"

"So I did, I remember now, but little good it will do us here. My son, you must leave me. If, perchance, you find a good Samaritan, you can return for me. If not, let me perish. It will sweeten the thought of death, to know that you live. Go, my son, go at once."

"I will never leave you," replied the boy firmly. "If die you must, I will die with you. But, father, we need not die. Have courage! All will yet be well."

Mr. Middleton could only groan in reply.

"Come, father," continued the boy, "we cannot stay here, we must be going."

"Go? Where can we go?" replied Mr. Middleton, bitterly.

He had entirely given up hope, and the cold was striking to his very bones. Lawrence also was shivering with the cold. His sodden garments clung to him like so much ice, but the brave boy made no complaint. Not for the world would he let his father know he was suffering. His only words were of cheer and comfort. Yielding to his entreaties, Mr. Middleton struggled to his feet. For the time being the child was the man; the man was the child, to obey. The bank of the river on that side was thickly wooded, and the darkness was intense. They could advance only by carefully feeling their way, and their progress was necessarily slow. The wind had arisen, and was sweeping through the tree-tops singing a lamentation and shaking the dying leaves down upon them in showers. They had not gone far before Mr. Middleton's feet were torn and bleeding, and his body had received many a painful wound. Where the flesh was torn the smarting of the tar was intolerable. Lawrence shielded him as much as possible by going in front, but his steps grew more and more faltering. At last he sat down on a log, and gave up in despair.

"This is the end," he exclaimed in a voice choking with emotion. "My son, my dear son, you must go on and leave me. Go! Go! I command you."

Lawrence put his arms around his father's neck caressingly. "Father, don't command me," he pleaded tearfully. "Don't make me disobey you. Could I ever live and be happy, if I should leave you here to die?"

"My boy, my precious brave boy, for your sake I will make one more effort," and with Lawrence's assistance, Mr. Middleton struggled to his feet. Every step was agony, he tottered from weakness, but he struggled on.

Suddenly, Lawrence cried, "Father, it shows light through the trees; we are getting out of the woods." And so it proved.

They soon came to a road, and in the distance a light twinkled.

"See, father, see!" cried the boy joyously, "a light; it must come from a house."

Before Mr. Middleton could answer, he stepped on a sharp stone, which pierced his foot, and he sank down in a dead faint.

"Father! Father!" cried Lawrence in alarm; but there was no answer.

A great terror come over him. Was his father dead? He knelt by his side, crying, begging him to speak to him, but his cries fell on deaf ears. He put his ear to his father's heart. No, he was not dead, for the heart was beating faintly. But one thought filled the mind of the boy. He must get help; his father must not die. Springing to his feet, he ran with all his strength toward the light. Would he never reach it? It seemed as far off as ever, and his breath was coming in quick gasps. At length he drew near, and to his joy, he saw that the light was streaming through the window of a large house. Just before he reached the door, he heard the swift beating of a horse's hoofs coming from the opposite direction. A horseman drew rein before the house, and without dismounting, called for the proprietor to come out. In answer to the summons, a white-haired, distinguished-looking gentleman came to the door. The man on horseback took off his hat, and bowing said, " Good-evening, Judge, I hope I see you well."

The gentleman addressed as Judge, came out on the veranda and said, "Why, is that you, Dryden?

It is so dark I did not know you. Anything special? Won't you dismount and come in?"

"Thank you, Judge, but I must be getting home. Just thought I would stop and tell you the news. The boys have been having a heap of fun this evening."

"Why, how is that?" asked the Judge.

"Oh! they caught a North Methodist preacher, on his way to Kansas, and that he might enter the Territory properly clothed, they gave him a fine coat of tar and feathers."

When Lawrence heard these words, his heart sank. He had come to the house of his enemies. He stopped, and cowered beneath a tree. He would hear more of what the man had to say.

"Were you in the scrape, Dryden?" Lawrence thought the Judge's voice was rather cold and hard, as he asked the question.

"I was there," answered Dryden, "but merely looked on, and enjoyed the fun. Bill Ketcham bossed the job."

The Judge shook his head. "I hardly like it, Dryden," he said. "The Northern papers get hold of these things, and make the most of them. Was the preacher alone?"

"No, he had a little boy with him."

"What became of the boy?"

Dryden hesitated before he answered, then

he said: "That is the part I don't like, and I will make a clean breast of it. I know you won't like it, but it can't be helped now. You see when Ketcham went to apply the tar to his father, the little fellow flew at him, and fastened his teeth in his wrist like a dog. It was a bad bite, and it made Ketcham so mad, he picked the boy up and threw him in the river."

"And you stood there, and let the boy drown?" The Judge's voice took on a metallic ring.

"Not so bad as that, Judge. But when the boy was thrown into the river, the preacher made a break and fought like a madman. It took some time to subdue him, and when the boys had him good and fast once more, they went to look for the boy, but he was nowhere to be seen. I really don't know whether he got out or was drowned."

"And the preacher, where is he now?" The Judge seemed to want to know all about it.

"Judge, when the boys got through with him, he was the funniest sight I ever saw. Some of the boys wanted to finish the job by hanging him, but they compromised the matter by tying him to a log, and sending him adrift down the river."

"Do you mean to say that you sent the man bound to a log, perfectly helpless, adrift?" asked the Judge in a surprised tone.

"That is about it, Judge."

"Do you not know it would have been more merciful to kill him outright?"

"That's so, Judge, but blast the nigger-stealing hypocrite, I don't know as he got more than he deserved."

"It's bad business, Dryden, and I am sorry you were in it. I am not surprised at Ketcham. To tell the truth, I am heartily sick of this border warfare. It cannot keep up forever without embroiling the whole country. Then the Union of States will be at an end, and war will come in earnest."

"Let it come! Damn the Union, anyway," growled Dryden. "What do we care for the money-grabbing Yankees? The sooner the South breaks away from the Union, the better. The dirty mudsills would n't dare to show fight; and if they did, we would whip them to a finish in sixty days."

"I sometimes think," said the Judge, "that if the South were allowed to withdraw from the Union peacefully, it would be the best thing that could happen; but if war comes, you will find no sixty-day job. However, we will not discuss the subject now. I am sorry you did not let the preacher go in peace. But what is done cannot be helped. Good-night, Dryden." And the Judge turned around to go into the house.

"Good-night, Judge," called Dryden as he rode away, but as he passed Lawrence the boy heard him mutter, " The Judge don't seem well pleased over the way we used the preacher. He is always talking about ' the majesty of the law.' Hang the law, as far as abolition preachers are concerned."

CHAPTER II

A GOOD SAMARITAN

"A BAD business! A bad business!" muttered Judge Lindsly, for that was the gentleman's name, as Dryden rode away, "I wonder what has become of that preacher and that little boy. I do hope he was not drowned."

He was soon to know what had become of them, for just as he was opening the door to enter the house, a small boy rushed up the steps, and falling at his feet, cried:

"Oh, sir, I heard what you said to that dreadful man! You are good, I know you are good. You will help father. He is dying — dying all alone. Come quick!"

Lawrence could say no more, for he was sobbing as if his heart would break.

"Bless me! bless me! what now?" ejaculated the surprised Judge, and he threw open the door. As the light streamed out, he was astonished to see a small boy, with wet and bedraggled garments, grovelling at his feet.

"Why! why! this must be the boy Dryden told about," exclaimed the Judge, in surprise. "Get up, my boy, and tell me about it."

"My father! my father!" sobbed Lawrence. "Oh! sir, won't you help him?"

The Judge reached down, and kindly raised Lawrence to his feet. "Why, my boy, you are dripping wet, and shivering with cold. Come into the house."

"Oh, no, no! My father, sir!"

"Where is your father?"

"Back here in the road. He is dying — dying all alone. Come quick!"

The Judge drew Lawrence into the house, and with a few questions learned from him the main points of his story.

Mrs. Lindsly, a stately, white-haired lady, looked on Lawrence with compassion. "The poor boy," she said. "What are you going to do, Judge?"

"Do? Do what I can to help those in need," answered the Judge. "But, Caroline, if what Dryden said is true, it will not do to have the man brought in here. I will have him taken to one of the negro cabins. The cabin of Susan and Uncle Jo will be just the place."

Then turning to Lawrence, the Judge said, "My poor boy, I will do all I can. Come with me." Taking his hat and cane, the Judge passed out into the night, and made his way to one of the negro cabins, where he tapped lightly at the door. It was opened by a buxom negro woman, one who had grown gray in the service of the family.

Seeing Judge Lindsly, she started back in surprise, and exclaimed, " De good Lawd! Is dat you, Massa Lindsly? What 's de mattah? Is de missy sick? "

" No, Susan, but a poor man is in trouble. Is Jo in? "

" Dar he is," said Susan, pointing to an aged negro who sat nodding by the fire, toasting his shins. " Dat good-for-nothin' nigger is gettin' lazier ebery day. Heah, Jo, Massa Lindsly wants you."

The patriarchal-looking negro hurriedly arose, and stood bowing, and pulling a lock of his white woolly hair.

" Susan, I have work for you and Jo both," said the Judge. " A white preacher has been roughly used by some of the boys — in fact tarred and feathered. This little boy says he is dying out here in the road. I am going to have him brought in here."

Susan raised her hands in horror. " Tar and feather a preacher ob de Gospel," she screamed. " Oh, Lawd! what de world comin' to? "

" He is a North Methodist preacher, Susan, one of those zealous fellows who are making all the trouble over in Kansas. He says you ought to be free."

" What! I and Jo po' miserable free niggers 'stead of belongin' to you, Massa Lindsly? " exclaimed Susan indignantly. " Go 'long, Massa, don't want anything to do wid him."

"But you must, Susan. You and Jo have a kettle of water heated by the time we get back. Now, Jo, stir yourself."

"Yes, yes, Massa," answered Jo, as he shuffled away to do his bidding.

During this colloquy, Lawrence stood impatiently by. "Please, hurry," he kept saying.

"Who dat boy?" asked Susan, now noticing him for the first time.

"He is the son of the preacher," answered the Judge.

"He all wet. He looks as if he bin in de ribber," said Susan, her sympathy aroused.

"He has, but do as I bid you. We will see to the boy afterwards," said the Judge.

The Judge now went and aroused two more of his slaves, Jake and George, stalwart fellows, who were told to get a lantern, and to go with Lawrence, to bring in a man that they would find, who had fainted by the roadside. At the same time the Judge despatched another slave in posthaste for a doctor. It was an excited boy who guided the two slaves to where his father lay.

Mr. Middleton had revived from his fainting spell while Lawrence was gone, and had crawled to one side of the road. He had called to Lawrence, but receiving no reply, knew he had gone for help. He thought he was dying, and his prayer was that his son might return in time to receive his dying blessing. Soon he heard hurried footsteps, and saw the flash of a lantern. But they would have passed him if he had not faintly called.

In an instant Lawrence was kneeling by his side. "I am here, father, I am here," he exclaimed joyfully, "and with help."

"Fo' de Lawd!" said George. "Is dat a man? I thought it was a big white stone."

In fact Mr. Middleton looked little like a human being.

The negroes raised Mr. Middleton in their stalwart arms, but Lawrence had hard work to make them do so. They could hardly be persuaded that the object at their feet was a man; it must be an evil spirit, and the boy an imp to entice them to their destruction. Their teeth fairly chattered with fear.

Lawrence had to explain what had happened, before he could get them to touch his father.

"What did dey tar and feather him fo'?" asked George.

"Because he said slavery was wrong," said Lawrence. "Because he was the friend of the black men, and said they ought to be free."

"Is he like John Brown in Kansas?" asked George, much interested. "John Brown, he friend of black man. Massa Lindsly, he good massa, but George would like to be free, just like white man."

"Yes," answered Lawrence, "father is just like John Brown. He is a friend of the black man. It is for this that the mob used him as they did."

To these simple-minded slaves Lawrence could have said nothing that would have aroused their sympathy more. Living on the border as they did, they had heard of John Brown, and looked upon him as their saviour. This man was like John Brown, and for their sakes he had suffered; and their fear turned to reverence. Tenderly they raised him in their arms and carried him as easily as if he had been a child. Lawrence walked by his father's side carrying the lantern, and encouraging him by telling him what a good man he had found.

Judge Lindsly was waiting for them, and as he looked at Mr. Middleton, he exclaimed, "Great God! why did n't they kill him at once!" And without ceremony he conducted them to the little cabin of Susan and Jo. But when Susan caught a glimpse of the burden which Jake and George bore, she gave a scream, and retreated to the rear of the cabin.

"Tak it away, Massa Lindsly, tak it away. It's no man; it's de Debbel, an' he git po' Susan," she yelled. "Good Massa Lindsly, tell him to go away."

"Don't be foolish, Susan," said the Judge, "this is no devil. It's a man, a preacher at that. You must do what you can for him."

But it was not until the Doctor came, and Mr.

Middleton had been relieved of some of his covering, that Susan became fully convinced she was not entertaining His Satanic Majesty. Fortunately the Doctor arrived almost as soon as his patient. He looked at Mr. Middleton, and then at the Judge, and in spite of himself, a smile came over his face. He was a fleshy, jolly man, and his whole countenance radiated good humor.

"The boys did a splendid job," he managed to whisper to the Judge; "but the man is thoroughly exhausted, and this may be serious."

He at once set to work with a will to do what he could. He first administered a stimulant and then went to work to remove the feathers and tar as best he could. He clipped Mr. Middleton's hair close to his head, and this left the head clean. "It is fortunate," said the Doctor, "that they spared the face."

It was not a hard job to divest Mr. Middleton of most of the feathers, but the tar was a different matter.

"It is a good thing," said the Doctor, "that the tar has not been on long enough to dry. If it had been, it would have been a most difficult job to remove it. Here, Susan, you and Jo lend a hand, and we will get off what we can. There, there be careful," as he noticed that Mr. Middleton winced under the operation. "Keep up courage, my friend. It hurts, but we will have you looking a little more respectable after a while. Mercy! but they did put it on thick."

Thus the Doctor worked away, keeping up a fire of small talk. Seeing that Mr. Middleton was growing very weak, he said, "There, that will do now. It will be a good long time before we get it all off." He then thoroughly anointed his patient with oil. "The oil," he remarked, "will keep the tar from drying." As he noticed the lacerated feet, he shook his head. "This is bad, bad," he said. "It will be some time before you can walk, my dear sir. Thank the Lord you have fallen in such good hands as my friend's, Judge Lindsly's here."

Having carefully dressed the wounded feet, the Doctor said, "Now for bed, and quiet."

Aunt Susan nearly fainted when she saw them placing Mr. Middleton in her nice clean bed, for Susan was a pattern for neatness.

"Never mind, Susan," said the Judge. "I will see that you have a brand new bed; but for the time being I am afraid you will have to give up the cabin, and go and live with Chloe. During the day, you must come and nurse Mr. Middleton; and Jo must see to him through the night."

It was with grumbling that Susan consented to this plan.

During all this time, Lawrence had scarcely been noticed. But now that his patient had been disposed of, the Doctor said to the Judge, "And this little fellow, does he also need my attention? Where did he come from?"

"My! I almost forgot the boy," said the Judge. And then he told the story of the affair as he had heard it, and how Lawrence had come to him for aid. "But," he added, "I have not yet heard how he rescued his father from the river."

"A brave boy, a brave boy," said the Doctor. "I must hear his full story one of these days."

Calling Lawrence to him, he patted him on the head, and said, "And now, my little man, what can we do for you?"

"Nothing, sir, only let me stay with father," replied Lawrence.

"Nothing?" laughed the Doctor. "I should reckon from your looks you at least needed dry, clean clothes."

"Bless me!" exclaimed the Judge, "we must not let him suffer."

A suit of clothes, about three sizes too large, was found. "It is an old suit that one of my grandsons discarded when visiting me last summer," said the Judge, "but it will do until we can get his own suit cleaned and pressed."

Lawrence felt much better when his wet clothes were off, even if the suit he put on was a misfit. A nourishing meal was also given him, and while the little fellow had not realized it until the food was placed before him, he was very hungry. Mr. Middleton was also given a little soup. Then the Doctor administered an opiate, and his patient was soon asleep.

"There," said the Doctor, "I think he will rest until morning."

In the meantime, a pallet had been spread on the floor for Lawrence, and he was soon sleeping the sweet sleep of childhood. As for Jo, he was to sit in his chair and watch over both.

The good Doctor now prepared to take his leave saying he would call again in the morning. But when alone with Judge Lindsly, he exploded and laughed until his fat sides shook. "Excuse me, Judge," he exclaimed, when he could get his breath, "but I can't help it. I never saw a more comical sight than that preacher. Yet I pity the poor devil."

"He certainly was a sight to behold," said the Judge. "Do you think, Doctor, that his treatment will endanger his life?"

"It may. His nervous system must have received a severe shock. He was also very roughly handled, and his feet are badly cut and bruised. As for the tar, that would have been a serious business if it had dried. As it is, I reckon I can get it all off in time. How did you come to get hold of him as soon as you did, Judge?"

The Judge told the story of the mob as related by Dryden, also how Lawrence had come to him.

The Doctor slapped his thigh. " By Jove! Judge," he exclaimed, "that is a boy worth having. I like his looks, and he has a bright, clear eye. He must be clean grit, too. Bit Ketcham, did he? And the brute tried to drown him. I wonder how the little fellow managed to rescue his father. But, Judge, now that you have the preacher and his son on your hands, what are you going to do with them?"

"I must keep them until the preacher gets well enough to travel, I suppose, but this will not increase my popularity in the county. You know there is some grumbling, because I will not endorse all that is being done to make Kansas a slave State,— the outrages on the ballot box for instance, and the violence used."

The Doctor reflected a moment. " You are certainly doing what few men in Platte County would do," he replied. "But, Judge, your kindness and philanthropy are so well known, they may let it pass. Why, Judge, you would n't let a yellow dog suffer."

"Yes, but you must remember that just now yellow dogs are more popular in Platte County than abolition Methodist preachers," replied the Judge grimly.

"You are right. I may even be roundly cursed for taking his case. But, Judge, we will stand together. Let Bill Ketcham peep, and I will give him a dose that he will remember. As for that boy, he is worth protecting, even if his father is n't. But I must be going. Good-night, Judge, I will be over in the morning," and the Doctor rode away.

The Judge mused a moment, and then entered the house where he found his wife anxiously awaiting him. After he had told her all, she said, "Did n't you do a foolish thing in befriending that man as you have done? You know the feeling of the community."

"I know, Caroline," answered the Judge, "but I could not let him die like a dog. And that boy!— it would have taken a heart of stone to withstand his pleading."

"Yes, that is so," said Mrs. Lindsly. "I was as anxious for you to go as you were to go, when I listened to his pitiful plea. I hope it will turn out all right"; but the good woman sighed as she said it.

In the morning, Dr. Goodnow found his patient feverish and very weak, but with no dangerous symptoms. "He will pull through, but it will take some days before he will be able to travel," he told the Judge.

There was great excitement among the slaves when it became known what had happened during the night. Jake and George, who had gone after Mr. Middleton, and Jo, to whose cabin he had been taken, whenever they had a chance to talk, had to tell their story, over and over again.

As for Jo, he was in his element. "You jest

ought to hab seen dat preacher," he would chuckle. "Susan thought he was de Debbel, an' she jest yell, as if de ole Ebel One had her. Dat preacher was all covered wid feathers, an' a great bunch on his haid. De doctah, he had to shave his haid,— no hair now. An' we had to pick de feathers off him."

Here Jo would stop and double up with laughter. "I jest hab to laugh," he would explain; "it was like pickin' a great big turkey."

But it was not only on the plantation of Judge Lindsly that the affair created excitement. The news of the lynching, and that the victim had been cared for by Judge Lindsly, spread over the county like wildfire. A few commended the Judge, but the great majority shook their heads, and said he ought to have let the preacher die. Some of the mob went so far as to say the same dose given the preacher ought to be dealt out to the Judge. But very few upheld Ketcham's attempt to drown the boy, and when he was upbraided for it he replied, "Fudge! I knew the little devil could swim."

Lawrence became quite a hero in the eyes of the people, who, above everything else, admire bravery, and many called to see him.

As the days passed, the whisperings against the Judge became mutterings. It became known that the Judge was not only caring for the preacher, but that he had taken him into his house, and was treating him as an honored guest. Then the mutterings became more threatening, and it needed but a word to fan the slumbering fire into open flame.

For a week, Mr. Middleton's condition remained about the same; after that, under the skilful treatment of Doctor Goodnow, he began to mend rapidly. For the first few days, beyond seeing he had good care, Judge Lindsly paid but little attention to his guest. What he did he felt to be his duty, but he had no desire to cultivate a close acquaintance. It was the Doctor who brought about a change.

"Judge, this is no ignorant, fanatical Methodist preacher you have on your hands," he remarked one day, "but a man of fine education, and rare attainments. And that boy, I tell you, has the making of a man in him. It is almost a pity to keep them down there in that slave cabin."

After he had gone, the Judge resolved to visit Mr. Middleton and see what the Doctor saw in him that led him to speak as he did. The result of that visit was that both Mr. Middleton and Lawrence were moved to the house, and to all appearances became welcome guests of their host. The Judge, as the Doctor had said, found Mr. Middleton, not only a man of high education, but a pleasing and interesting conversationalist, and they enjoyed many a talk together.

"How is it," asked the Judge one day, "that a man of your education and refinement came wandering through Missouri as you did, on your way to Kansas?"

"It is but just to you, Judge," answered Mr. Middleton, "that you should know a little of my past history. As you surmise, I have a collegiate education. For some years I was a professor in the University of N——. Then I took a pastorate, and until two years ago I was the pastor of one of the largest Methodist churches in Ohio. At that time my wife was taken from me. The blow nearly killed me. I lost interest in church work, and resigned my pastorate. Then came this Kansas trouble, and I heard that many of our church members had migrated thither, and were without a shepherd. I offered my services to the aid society, and they were gladly accepted. I thought that a change would arouse my flagging energies and do me good."

"You certainly have had excitement enough to arouse the energies of a nearly dead man," remarked the Judge, with a smile.

"Yes, it has been strenuous enough to suit me," answered Mr. Middleton. "But to continue. I could not bear to leave my little boy behind, so I brought him along. I started with a good horse and buggy. Unfortunately I did not fully understand the feeling in your State, and entered it too far south. In fact I ought to have kept out of Missouri entirely, and gone through Iowa. But by being careful I had little trouble until I reached the northern part of Clay County. A couple of days before I encountered the mob here, I drove into a small village where a political meeting was in progress. There were a great many drunken men around, and before I was aware of it, the buggy was surrounded by a crowd who demanded who I was, and where I was going. I evaded them by telling them I was going to St. Joseph, which was true, as I wished to make that city.

"'He talks like a Northerner,' yelled one, and I had to admit I was from Ohio.

"'Who are you for, for President?' yelled another. I told them I was not in politics, and did not expect to vote for any one; in fact could not, as I should not be a legal voter anywhere.

"'Hurrah for Buchanan!' they shouted, 'Hurrah for Buchanan! Show your colors!'

"I suppose I was foolish, but this I absolutely refused to do. It seemed to me almost like denying my Saviour. The first I knew, I was surrounded by a howling mob, my buggy was overturned and smashed, my baggage was scattered to the four winds, and my horse was frightened and ran away, and that was the last I saw of him.

"I was saved from bodily injury by some cooler heads, but told to leave the town at once. That evening Lawrence and I slept in the woods. I had a little over four hundred dollars with me. This money I divided, sewing half of it in my boy's coat, and keeping the other half myself. What I gave the boy is fortunately saved. I think some of those who mobbed me must have followed on horseback, and got ahead, arousing the mob I met at Platte River, for I was suddenly surrounded, and those who composed the mob seemed to know who I was, and what had happened to me."

"It was very foolish your attempting to reach Kansas by coming the route you did," said the Judge. "It is a wonder you were not mobbed sooner. The country you came through is as intensely Southern as Mississippi. You were wise in dividing your money with the boy."

"Yes, and I want you to do me a favor, Judge. Will you not take some of that money, and buy me a decent outfit of clothes? Lawrence also must have a full outfit. You know I am wearing your clothes now."

"And they fit you very well," answered the Judge laughing, "but I will see to the clothes."

The Judge was as good as his word. He went to Platte City the next day, and purchased full outfits for both Mr. Middleton and Lawrence.

"How can I ever reward you for your kindness?" said Mr. Middleton with emotion, as the parcels were delivered. "But, Judge, there is another matter of which I wish to speak. Lawrence tells me some of your neighbors are very angry because you are harboring us. He overheard two men talking to-day. He was in the woods looking for nuts, and they came and stood close to where he was. He could not understand all that they said, but he understood enough to know there is mischief brewing. One of them said you ought to be given the same medicine that the preacher got. Then they whispered, and one of them said out loud, 'We will hang him next time.' "

The Judge looked grave. "You need not fear for me," he said, "but I am afraid that last remark applied to you. Do not be alarmed at what I tell you. I know that there are two or three men trying to stir up another mob to come and take you by force and hang you. They have not succeeded so far, but the election is close at hand, and the people are greatly excited. A spark, a trivial circumstance, may cause an explosion. I think it best that as soon as you are able to travel, I find means of getting you over to Kansas."

"Why not send me right away?" asked Mr. Middleton anxiously.

"You are not yet able to ride, much less walk," answered the Judge. "Within a week will be time enough."

But incidents were happening of which neither knew, toward hastening the departure of Mr. Middleton, and in a way that neither suspected.

William Ketcham had made a discovery which

greatly alarmed him. At the time Mr. Middleton was mobbed, it will be remembered that he was stripped. Ketcham took charge of his clothes. Only a few dollars were found in the pockets and a package of letters.

"Keep the money, Bill," said one, "and pay for the expense of this show. Then when we get together again you can set them up."

"Might as well keep the clothes, too," said Ketcham, "it looks like a pretty good suit."

So when he went away, he carried the suit with him. He threw it aside and did not think of it for some days, but noticing it one day he thought he would examine it.

"A blamed good suit; as good as I ever wore," he soliloquized. "I wonder if it will fit me."

As he talked he ran his hand over the coat. He thought he heard a rustle, and surely the coat was thicker in one place than elsewhere. He examined the seam closely, and it had the appearance of having been opened and only roughly closed. To re-open the seam was the work of a moment, and he was rewarded in his search by finding two hundred dollars in bills.

"You are a lucky man, William Ketcham," he chuckled. "The boys need know nothing of this. Reckon I will open this bunch of letters now, I may find something in them."

He looked at one, and then another and cast them

aside with a contemptuous grunt. But at last he came to one that made him start in surprise, for in it he saw his own name. He read and reread it, and as he did so, great drops of sweat stood out on his forehead.

"That preacher must die," he muttered. "Fool that I was not to hang him when I had him in my power. Came here to spy on me, did he? Well, I will fix him."

Folding up the letter he sought one of his pals, one that he could trust.

"Read that, Bob," he said, as he placed the letter in his hands.

Bob Travers took the letter, and this is what he read:

My Dear Middleton :—

I understand you are starting for Kansas in a few days, and on the score of old friendship, I ask you to do a little detective work for me while there. I shall be in Kansas myself by the close of the year, but cannot go now.

I do not know as you are aware that sometime ago I had a brother brutally murdered in Kansas. As near as I can learn, the name of the murderer was William Ketcham, but so far he has escaped justice owing to the unhappy condition of that territory. Enclosed I send you all the facts in the case as far as I know. If possible, will you not try to find out more of the facts, and where this Ketcham can be found; for when I come I will have justice, if it can be had in this world. I hope to see you before the close of the year.

Yours ever,   Charles Canfield.

Travers gave a low whistle as he finished the letter.

"You know all about it, Bob, you were with me," said Ketcham.

"Yes, and gave you thunder for shooting the fellow. It was about as useless a killing as I ever saw, but for your sake I swore it was in self-defence."

"The officer who investigated seemed to be satisfied," replied Ketcham doggedly.

"Yes, because he was one of our kind. Took my word, and refused to call other witnesses. Then you remember we greased him to the tune of five hundred. Bill, if that affair is ever probed to the bottom it will go hard with you."

"You haven't gone back on me, have you, Bob?"

"Not by a long shot. What a pity we did n't hang that preacher when we had him."

"It is not too late yet," responded Ketcham with an oath.

"How are you going to get him when he is under old Lindsly's wing?" asked Travers.

"Take him, take him by force, and if Lindsly objects, let him take the consequences."

"But will the boys be with you?" inquired Travers.

"I can rally thirty in twenty-four hours, if need be. How are you, Bob?"

"Put it there," said Travers, extending his hand. And the two men shook hands.

"When the preacher is out of the way," continued Ketcham, "we will look out for this Canfield when he comes, and see that he makes no trouble."

"The quicker we get the preacher out of the way the better," said Travers. "When will it be?"

"Not until we get back from Kansas," answered Ketcham. "You know we have a raid all planned for to-morrow night."

"That's so. Well, we can attend to the preacher as we come back. Do it all up in one job, as it were," said Travers with a laugh.

The raid was made as planned, but in some way the settlers had been informed of their coming, and the raiders met with a warm reception, being driven back with the loss of one killed and two wounded. One of the wounded was Ketcham, who had received a ball through the hand, the same hand that had applied the tar to Mr. Middleton.

He was insane with rage, and no sooner had the band reached Missouri soil than he called a halt.

"Boys, there is a traitor somewhere," he exclaimed. "Those settlers must have been informed of our coming, or they could never have gathered in such force."

"Pint the traitor out, and he will swing from a tree," growled one of the gang.

"I know who it is," cunningly continued Ketcham, "but it is none of the boys; it 's that preacher Middleton that Judge Lindsly is harboring. I received warning he was a spy, but paid little attention to it."

"How could he get the news across the river?" asked one.

"Oh! that 's easy," said Ketcham, "that precious boy of his is always sneaking around, and he is thick with the slaves. Judge Lindsly is easy, you know, with his niggers. Never knows where they are nights."

"Let 's hang the preacher, anyway, to pay for poor Dick Sales. A nice figure we cut, sneaking back from Kansas with one dead, and two wounded," spoke up another of the gang. "But what if the Judge shows fight?"

"He dare not," said Ketcham, "when he sees our numbers. He may bluster for a time, but he will give the preacher up when it comes to the scratch."

"I don't know about that," spoke up Travers, "the Judge has lots of sand."

"We'll take the preacher, anyway," growled Ketcham, "and if the Judge gets hurt, it will be his own fault. What do you say, boys?"

"Agreed! We are just aching for a little necktie party, anyway," they shouted. "Lead on, Bill."

Well satisfied with his success, Ketcham said, "All right, boys, but no flinching! Come on!"

The gang started in high glee. To them to hang an abolitionist was the height of sport. Just before they reached their destination, they halted and held a consultation as to the best manner of proceeding. It was decided that at first, only three or four of the gang should show themselves, and try to get hold of the preacher by surprise or strategy. If this failed, the whole gang would come and take Mr. Middleton by force.

Ketcham, accompanied by three of his men, rode up to the residence of Judge Lindsly. As the weather was mild for the time of year, to their chagrin they found the Judge sitting on his porch. Surprise was impossible.

"Howdy, Judge?" said Ketcham pleasantly.

"Quite well, thank you," replied the Judge. "What can I do for you, gentlemen? Will you not dismount? I have just been making some fine cider; perhaps you gentlemen would like to test it."

"Cider is a mighty thin drink, Judge," replied Ketcham with a laugh, as he threw himself from his horse.

"Well, perhaps I can find something stronger," answered the Judge. "What do you say to some fine old bourbon?"

"Just the thing, Judge. Just the thing," replied the delighted Ketcham. "What do you say, boys?"

"It suits us," answered the three as they smacked

their lips. The Judge's bourbon was famous throughout the county.

Judge Lindsly stepped into the house, and spoke to a servant. When he came out, it was noticed he took a position close to the door. Soon a neat looking colored girl came out with a tray on which were glasses and a decanter. Each of the four took a couple of drinks.

"I say, Judge, that 's the real stuff," remarked Ketcham. "Whar did you get it?"

"Direct from old Kentucky," replied the Judge. "I am glad you like it."

"Nothing like good ol' bourbon," continued Ketcham, looking at his empty glass wistfully. "I say, Judge, if those blamed abolitionists of the North would drink more bourbon, thar would not be so many of them."

The conversation now lagged for a while. It was hard for Ketcham to state his business to so courteous a host. At last he said: "By the way, Judge, how is that preacher we had the fun with, getting along?"

"Improving slowly," answered the Judge coldly.

"Judge, we know your kindness of heart, and honor you for it," continued Ketcham softly, "but that fellow is imposing on you."

"How it that?" asked the Judge. "He does not profess to be anything but what he is."

"Don't be too sure. I have evidence, positive evidence, that the fellow is a spy, a mean, sneaking spy, and he is here in the pay of the abolitionists to spy upon us."

"How did you find that out?" The Judge's voice was colder than ever.

Ketcham hesitated, then replied, " I do not mind telling you we are just back from a raid in Kansas to break up a band of outlaws who have made it a business to come over here and steal our niggers. In some way, they found out we were coming, and gave us a warm reception. We are bringing back poor Dick Sales dead."

" How about you? I see you have your hand in a sling." There was a tinge of sarcasm in the voice of the Judge when he asked the question.

"Oh! they plugged me through the hand, but it is not much. But to come to the point. We have found out for sure that it was the preacher who sent the word we were coming."

"He? How could that be?" asked the Judge in surprise. "To my certain knowledge he has not been out of his room."

"How about that sneaking boy of his?" asked Ketcham. "That little chap is sharp. He found it out, told his father, and no doubt, one of the slaves carried the news over, and got back before morning."

" My slaves are not bearers of such news," replied

the Judge. "Ketcham, this story is but a subterfuge. Why beat around the bush? The facts are, you fellows have made a raid over in Kansas, got beaten, and come back sore; and now want your revenge out on Middleton. What do you propose to do with him, if I give him up?"

"Hang him," blurted out Ketcham. "The boys are wild over the death of Sales, and nothing else will satisfy them."

",You can't have him, and the quicker you get out of here the better." There was no mistaking the voice of the Judge. He was terribly in earnest.

"Judge, I am sorry," said Ketcham. "We don't want to hurt you, but that man we must have. I don't blame you for making a show of resistance, but you see the folly of making a fight. Better give him up peaceably."

With this he attempted to enter the house, but was astounded to find himself confronted by the Judge, and looking into the muzzle of a revolver.

"Another step and you are a dead man," said the Judge coolly.

Ketcham recoiled, and took a step backward. "Judge, do you mean this?" he asked, astounded.

"I certainly mean it. There! don't you attempt to draw a gun, or any of your companions. If you do, I fire. Now face about, and get off the porch, and you and your companions make yourselves scarce, as soon as possible."

Just then the Judge felt a tug at his coat, and a childish voice said, " Please give me a pistol, too, Judge Lindsly."

Lawrence had heard the altercation, had come to the door, and at once had recognized the man who threw him into the river.

Without lowering his weapon or looking down, Judge Lindsly asked, "What do you want with a pistol, Lawrence?"

"To shoot that man," replied the boy pointing at Ketcham. "I hate him."

"This is no place for you. Go back into the house at once," commanded the Judge.

Lawrence reluctantly obeyed.

In the meantime Ketcham and his men had made a pretence of retiring, but instead the leader had made a signal to the rest of his gang, and they came galloping up, some fifteen in number.

Ketcham now turned back, and with a look of triumph on his face, cried, "You see you are out-numbered. We are going to have that preacher, even if we have to get him over your dead body. Be sensible, and let us have him peaceably."

"Never," replied the Judge through his set teeth, the gleam of battle in his eye.

What would have happened in the next moment would be hard to tell, if the Doctor had not come driving up in his gig. He looked upon the scene in

"Please give me a pistol, too, Judge Lindsly"

amazement. "Why! Why! What is this?" he exclaimed. "What does this mean?"

"It means that we have come for that cursed abolition preacher to hang him, and we are going to have him," replied Ketcham sullenly, "and don't you dare interfere, Doc."

"What does the Judge say?" asked the Doctor.

"He is fool enough to say he will defend the fellow to the death," growled Ketcham. "He will have a chance, if he does n't get a little more reasonable.

"So you thought I could n't kill the preacher quick enough, and concluded to take a hand," said the Doctor, with a laugh.

"That 's about it," replied Ketcham, hardly knowing how to take him.

"Look a-here, Bill," said the Doctor with a comical wink; "don't you know this is reflecting on me? Have you ever counted the number of my patients I have put under ground?"

"Never have, Doc," replied Ketcham, with a grin, "but there has been heaps of them."

"Just so, and yet you can't give me a little time with this preacher. It is n't fair, boys. Well, I admit the preacher is a tough proposition. You fellows tried to kill him and failed; I have tried it for nearly three weeks, and he is alive yet, so you think nothing will do but a rope."

" That 's about it, Doc," the crowd yelled.

"And the Judge here objects to this little necktie party," continued the Doctor.

"But we will have it, all the same," chorused the crowd.

"Well, well, the Judge never was much of a hand for fun, and I have always known him to be an obstinate man, but I reckon I can convince him. Hold steady, boys, until I try my hand. Don't let us have any blood-letting, if we can help it."

"Hurrah! Hurrah! the Doctor is with us," shouted the mob. "Now we are all right."

The Doctor went to his gig, and took from under the seat two wicked-looking revolvers. "These are beauties," said he; "they never miss fire, and I never miss the mark. - Now, boys, let me interview the Judge. I reckon I can persuade him to give up the preacher without trouble. If he kicks, these fellows will have a remarkably quieting effect on him until the job is done."

Thus saying, the Doctor made his way up the steps to the porch where the Judge stood. The mob noticed that the latter made no objection to the advance of the Doctor, but that he still kept his weapon levelled, so as to cover one of their number.

But no sooner did the Doctor reach the side of the Judge, than his whole demeanor changed. Turning he held a revolver cocked in each hand, and to his dismay Ketcham saw that the muzzle of one was pointed directly at his breast, and that the Doctor's finger rested on the trigger.

"Boys," the Doctor began, in a voice which did not show the least trace of excitement, "this farce has now gone far enough. I will give you just two minutes to get out of here. If one of you remains, at the end of that time, these fellows bark, and when they bark, as you well know, they bite. I shall count a hundred, by that time you must all be gone."

But he had not counted fifty before there was not a man left, and all that was seen of the mob was a cloud of dust disappearing down the road. "Judge," said he, as he turned to that personage, "that patient of mine seems to be giving you some trouble. I reckon it would be wise to ship him at once."

"Doctor, you are talking sense," answered the Judge; "but come in and let us finish the rest of that decanter."

CHAPTER III

THAT our young readers may fully understand this story, it may be necessary to give a few historical facts. For several years before the great Civil War, a cruel and relentless warfare raged along the borders of Kansas and Missouri.

From the very inception of our Government, up to the secession of the Southern States, slavery had been a bone of contention. At the adoption of the Constitution there was but one of the original thirteen States that did not hold slaves. The Northern States gradually abolished it, but it fastened itself on the Southern States with a grip of iron.

The Fathers of the Republic were in hope that slavery would gradually die out; and toward this end, when the great Northwest Territory was organized, out of which, afterwards, there were five States created, there was a proviso that it should be forever dedicated to freedom.

Missouri was admitted into the Union in 1820, and it wished to come in as a Slave State. It extended so far North that this was bitterly opposed by the free States, and the nation became greatly excited. This was the beginning of the struggle be-

tween freedom and slavery. At last a compromise
was effected. It was agreed that Missouri might
come in as a slave State, but that thereafter no slave
States should be admitted north of the parallel 36
degrees, 30 minutes. This line is what is known in
history as the Mason and Dixon Line.

In 1850, California was admitted into the Union
as a free State. The southern portion of it lies south
of the Mason and Dixon Line, and as it was admitted as a free State, the friends of slavery claimed
that the Compromise had been broken, and therefore should no longer be held as a law of the land.

To conciliate the South, the Fugitive Slave Law
was passed. This law compelled the people of the
North to become slave-hunters in case of runaway
slaves. So drastic were its provisions that a Southern writer and a friend of slavery says:

"Some of its provisions were not only inconsistent
with the civilization of the age, but required citizens of
Massachusetts, New York, and Ohio to do what no
self-respecting Virginian could have been forced to
do."

This law, as it should, produced righteous indig-
nation throughout the entire North.

About this time the Territories of Kansas and Ne-
braska began to be settled. Now began a political
contest memorable in the history of the nation, a
contest in which the great names of Lincoln and
Douglas became inseparably linked. The South was

determined to make Kansas a slave State. To accomplish this, the Missouri Compromise would have to be repealed.

Stephen A. Douglas, one of the greatest statesmen ever produced by this country, and known as the Little Giant, was an aspirant for the presidency. To realize the height of his ambition, he had to conciliate the South. He therefore advanced a doctrine known as "Squatter Sovereignty." It was that the citizens of each Territory should settle for themselves the question whether the Territory should come in as a free or a slave State.

Around this doctrine a political battle was fought in Congress, which stirred the country from centre to circumference. The advocates of "Squatter Sovereignty" won, and the Missouri Compromise was repealed.

In May, 1854, what was known as the Kansas-Nebraska Act was passed. This act provided that when these Territories asked to be admitted as States, they should come in as free or as slave States, as the citizens of the Territories themselves should decide.

Douglas fondly hoped that this would pacify the South, and forever settle the vexed question of slavery. But instead of settling the question, it opened a Pandora box, and the whole country was soon engaged in a bitter strife. A conflict began which raged with greater or less fury, until it culminated in the Civil War.

The question now was, Which side could bring the most immigrants into the Territory of Kansas? All over the North, especially in the New England States, aid societies were formed to assist, and to induce immigrants to settle in Kansas. Soon a stream of settlers from the North was pouring into that Territory. Many rough and adventurous spirits were among the immigrants, but the great majority were hardy, honest men whose purpose was to make a home. That many others went for the sole purpose of making Kansas a free State, there can be no doubt.

In this contest, the North had all the advantage. It was impossible for a slaveowner to avoid bankruptcy if he moved into Kansas with his slaves. The non-slaveowners of the South could not be induced to go. The large majority of these non-slaveowners were known in the South as "poor white trash," and lacked enterprise and ambition. It was not long before the South saw that it was playing a losing game. Ten Northern men to one Southern were going into the Territory.

The South now tried another and more desperate game. Right across the Missouri River from Kansas, lay the slave State of Missouri. In its border counties were organized bands of men known as

"border ruffians." They would try to accomplish by
force what they could not accomplish lawfully; they
would invade the Territory, drive the free-State
settlers from their homes, and in some cases murder
them in cold blood. At the time of an election, the
Missourians would come over in great numbers,
drive honest voters away from the polls, stuff the
ballot boxes, and fix the returns to suit themselves.
Pitched battles were fought, villages burned, and
innocent men massacred. Thus Kansas became
known as "Bleeding Kansas." But the outrages
were not all on one side. Desperadoes, for the purpose of plunder and revenge, would invade Missouri, burn houses, destroy or carry off property,
and run off slaves. Thus on both sides it was cruel,
barbarous war.

It is strange that such a warfare could continue
for years without embroiling the whole country.
But both North and South dreaded what both expected to come sooner or later — war between the
sections; and both sides wanted to put off the evil
day as long as possible. The blood shed in Kansas was but the precursor of the rivers of blood
which were to flow later for the preservation of the
Union.

During all the Kansas trouble, President Pierce
was a strong ally of the South. He did all in his
power to make Kansas a slave State. He was
bound heart and soul to the South, and willingly

did its bidding. He appointed governor after governor of the Territory, but they resigned in disgust when the National Government refused to protect the settlers in their honest rights, and upheld the acts of the Missourians.

It was during the height of this trouble that the Rev. Arthur Middleton was sent by an aid society in Ohio, to administer religious consolation to the settlers of the unhappy Territory.

CHAPTER IV

JOHN BROWN

AS the Judge and the Doctor sat sipping their toddy, they discussed the situation.

"You must get rid of that preacher as soon as possible," said the latter. "It is but a few days before election, and the excitement instead of subsiding will grow more intense. There is no telling what may happen. If Fremont be elected the deuce will be to pay. I honestly think the South will try to kick out of the Union, and I can't blame her much. Then, Ketcham and his gang will not give up so easily. You may look for another visit from them any time. Their being fooled this time will only anger them. I wonder what it is that makes Ketcham so anxious to hang Middleton. There must be something that we do not know."

"What you say, Doctor, is true," answered the Judge, "except as to the election of Fremont. I do not think there is any danger of that. The South will be solid for Buchanan, and enough Northern States will go for him to make his election sure. But as to Middleton and myself, there is real danger. We cannot always beat them off as easily as we did this time, nor can I always have Doctor

Goodnow by my side. Doc, but for you I might have been a dead man by this time, and Middleton hanging to a tree."

"Blast Middleton!" exclaimed the Doctor. "You are worth ten thousand of him. That you might lose your life defending him is not to be thought of."

Just then there was a tap at the door, and Lawrence came into the room.

"What is it, my boy?" asked the Judge.

"Father says he would like to see you and the Doctor, both," answered Lawrence.

"Very well. Tell him we will be up shortly," said the Judge, and then he asked the Doctor if he had noticed the boy by his side, as he drove up.

"I did, and wondered that you allowed him by you at such a time."

"I did not know he was there until he plucked me by the coat, and asked me for a pistol."

"A pistol? That beats me! Then he wanted to help you to fight, did he?"

"Yes, he said he wanted it to shoot Ketcham with, and pointed him out as the man who threw him into the river."

"Say, Judge, that boy is true blue. I wish we could ship the father, and keep the boy. He not only has true grit, but he is sharp as a tack. Wanted to shoot Ketcham, did he? Well, that is a good one!" and the Doctor shook with laughter.

"I am glad no harm came to him," said the

Judge. " But we had better go and see what Mr. Middleton wants."

" Yes. I wonder if he fully realizes the danger you are running in protecting him."

The preacher greeted them warmly as they entered. " First," said he, "I want to thank you two for what you have done for me. Not satisfied with what you had done, both of you have just risked your lives, that mine might be saved. It is written, 'Greater love hath no man than this, that a man lay down his life for his friends.' Surely you found me a stranger and took me in. May the choicest blessings of Heaven rest upon you both."

" The Judge surely deserves your thanks," said the Doctor, "but I do not, for I only practised my profession. It is a doctor's business to save life. To change the subject — how is my patient? "

" Getting along nicely. I feel quite strong, thanks to you, Doctor."

" Strong enough to travel, that is, to ride? " queried the Doctor.

" Yes; and the reason I sent for you, gentlemen, is to tell you I must go, and go at once. Lawrence has told me all that has happened. I had no idea I was bringing such danger on you. That you should risk your lives to save mine is almost past belief. Why should you? Better give me into the hands of the mob than that you should perish. I cannot, will not, subject you to another such peril as you have just passed through. I must leave your house, and at once. Judge Lindsly, you I can never repay. Doctor, for your kindness I can never pay, but for your professional services I can; for, as you know, I have a little money."

"Don't insult me," growled the Doctor. "But what I should like to know is, why it is that this man Ketcham pursues you so vindictively?"

"I cannot imagine," replied Mr. Middleton, "unless it is that just before I left Ohio, I received a letter from a friend saying he had a brother most foully murdered in Kansas, and from what he could learn, he was murdered by a man named William Ketcham. He wanted me to look up a few facts for him, saying that he himself would be out in a few weeks. That letter was in the pocket of the coat the mob stripped from me. Ketcham may have got hold of it."

"Ah! that explains all. He imagines you are here to spy on him. Judge, the case is more desperate than I thought. Mr. Middleton must be got away, and that to-night. That mob will come back at the first opportunity. And if they do," continued he, looking at Mr. Middleton quizzically, "you will travel to heaven by the rope route, as sure as you are born."

The preacher was a little shocked at the irreverence of the remark, but had to admit its truth.

"One word more, Mr. Middleton," said the Doctor, with a twinkle in his eye, "if we get you to Kansas safe and sound, you can report that all Missourians are not barbarians, as I reckon your Church thinks."

"I care not what the Church thinks," replied Mr. Middleton, "I know if I ever met any of God's people, I have met them right here."

"Better not tell that to John Brown," said the Doctor, with a laugh. "He preaches that any one who owns a slave is bound straight for perdition."

John Brown! John Brown! The preacher winced when he heard the name, for he remembered that when he left Ohio, he carried a letter of introduction to John Brown. It was in his baggage which was destroyed when his buggy was overturned. Well for the preacher that Ketcham did not get hold of that. If he had, nothing would have saved him. Not for the world would he have the good Doctor know he had had such a letter, so he contented himself by saying, "I have never met Brown, but I have heard of him."

"You will see him if you are in Kansas long," said the Doctor. "He thinks he has a divine commission to smite the slaveholders, even as the Hebrews smote the Canaanites."

"I hope my troubles will be over when I get to Kansas," said Mr. Middleton, wishing to change the subject, as he did not care to discuss John Brown.

"I reckon you may have your troubles when you

get there," dryly remarked the Doctor; "there are safer places than Kansas just now; but it is the Judge's and my business to see that you get there."

"I see that we have wearied Mr. Middleton," spoke up the Judge. "We had better let him rest, while we discuss ways and means of getting him away."

"I can be ready at any time; you see, my baggage is light," said the preacher.

"We will get you away to-night, just what time I can't say yet. Rest easy until we call for you."

"Are we really to go to Kansas?" asked Lawrence after the Judge and the Doctor had withdrawn.

"Yes, my boy, and I trust that our trials will soon be over." Little did he think what would happen before he had been in Kansas many days; and little did he think what would happen even before he started.

The Doctor and the Judge were soon in a deep discussion as to the best means of getting Mr. Middleton away.

"What he said about that letter," said the Doctor, "worries me. I know Bill Ketcham, and I know he will never let up until he has the preacher in his power. He pretends it was in one of the rows that he killed the man, and that he shot him in self-defence. But the fact is, he shot the fellow in cold blood to get his horse, which was a very fine one. He would have swung for it long ago, if it had not been for the disturbed condition of the country. Finding that letter has scared him."

"Then you think he will strike again soon?" said the Judge.

"Yes, and if I mistake not, before morning. Judge, there are but two ways for you to act: one is to rally your neighbors, and give Ketcham and his gang a warm reception when they come; the other is to get the preacher and the boy out of the house and away, so that when the gang do come, you can let them search the house and premises to their hearts' content. They will not dare touch you if you make no resistance."

"It must be the last plan," said the Judge. "I can never consent to the slaughter of my neighbors."

"Then," continued the Doctor, "let's see. I have it. No doubt there are spies watching the house this minute. As soon as it is dark, slip the preacher and the boy out of the back door. Let them go down the lane back of the negro quarters, until they come to that big walnut tree. I will meet them there, with two good saddle horses. Then by little-used roads that I know well, I will get them to the river. Once there, Abe Dilloh will put them across for me, and no questions asked."

"The plan is a good one, Doc," said the Judge, "and I will see it is followed to the letter. I shall breathe easier when they are gone."

Just then a man came riding up to the house on a reeking horse, and asked if Doc Goodnow was there.

The Doctor answered in person.

"Doc, you air wanted, and wanted quick. Pete Shockley has shot himself foolin' with an ole revolver, an' he is bad."

"This is unfortunate," said the Doctor in a low voice to the Judge. "I shall have to go, and I may not get back as soon as expected. But have the preacher and the boy at the rendezvous at the time set. Don't keep them in the house a moment after dark. Tell them to wait until I come." Thus saying, the Doctor got into his gig and rapidly drove away.

Hardly had he gone, when another messenger came inquiring for the Doctor. This time it was Jim Shephard who had been taken violently ill, and who wanted his services. The messenger looked much disappointed when told the Doctor had just been called away. The Judge did not like this man's actions. He seemed in no hurry to go, and was very inquisitive. At last he rode slowly away.

"I believe that last messenger was a fake," said the Judge,—"a plan to get the Doctor away from here."

But night came, and no sooner had darkness fallen, than Mr. Middleton and Lawrence, under the guidance of old Jo, slipped from the house. Mr.

Middleton was still quite weak and very lame, his mangled feet having not entirely healed yet, but in due time they reached the walnut; and there, after giving them many warnings Jo left them.

The hours slipped by, and midnight came, and still no Doctor; and from the house there came no alarm.

When Ketcham and his gang were well away from the scene of their defeat, they halted for a conference. They were wild with rage, and ready for any desperate deed.

"Boys, when this is known," exclaimed Ketcham, with a great oath, "we will be the laughingstock of the community. Twenty of us put to flight by two men!"

"On the other hand, if we had killed the Judge and the Doctor, the country would have been too hot to hold us," spoke up one.

"You are right, Tom," answered Ketcham, "but I will not be balked. Now, what is the best to do?"

After several of the gang had suggested this and that, Ketcham suddenly slapped his thigh, and said, "I have it, boys."

"What is it, Bill? What is it?" they cried all at once.

"First, we must get that Doctor away. We will send a messenger for him. Some one is very sick. Must have his services at once. That will leave only the Judge. He will hardly expect us back to-night. We will wait until about midnight, then disguise ourselves as raiders from Kansas, and demand admittance in the name of John Brown. The Judge will not fool with Brown, he knows his reputation too well. Once in the house, the rest is easy."

"Capital, Bill, capital! You ought to be a general," was the unanimous verdict.

First the messenger was sent to lure away the Doctor. One of the gang was to go home, and be taken violently sick. "Don't worry, boys," he said. "I will be the sickest man you ever saw, and keep the Doctor all night."

So the messenger was sent, but after a while he returned with the information that the Doctor had already been called away.

"That is just as well, even better, for he might have discovered that Jim was faking," said Ketcham.

The gang waited until about midnight, then disguised as Kansas raiders, rode boldly up to the residence of Judge Lindsly. The house was dark, and as far as appearances went, its inmates were asleep.

Ketcham thundered at the door. "Who is there?" asked the Judge, after a decent interval.

"John Brown. Open quick, or it will be the worse for you."

The Judge was astounded at the answer, but guessed rightly that it was Ketcham and his men, personating a raiding party from Kansas. But be-

fore he could unfasten the door, three or four shots
were heard, then a rapid fusillade, and shouts of
angry men.

Ketcham was as astounded as the Judge, as to
the meaning of the firing. He jumped from the
porch just in time to hear one of his men call out
he was wounded, and Ketcham became aware he
was being attacked by a large party.

"Back, men, back!" he shouted. "The Judge
has ambushed us. Damn him! he will pay for this."

It was but a moment before the gang were in
full retreat, leaving one of their number wounded
and another dead upon the field.

Not only the house, but the whole plantation, was
in an uproar. The negroes were crouching in their
cabins panic-stricken. What did that sudden fight
mean? The Judge was at a loss to know; but he
had little time to consider, for there came another
thunderous rap at the door, and then it was burst
in without ceremony, and a tall man with grizzly
hair and deep-set eyes stalked into the room.

"Who lives here?" he asked in a commanding
tone.

"I do," said the Judge, "and I should like to
know what this midnight attack means."

"It was you that attacked, not I," answered the
man, "and you shall pay for it. We do not murder
old men, women, or children, but out of the house,
for I shall order it to be fired immediately."

"Who are you, that you dare do this?" asked the Judge indignantly.

"I am John Brown," thundered the man. "No words! You and your family out of this house at once or I will burn it over your heads."

But just at this time there was an interruption; the Doctor rushed in, and a moment later Mr. Middleton came limping into the room. The Doctor had arrived at the place of rendezvous for Mr. Middleton, just as the firing commenced. He was startled. "Middleton, there is trouble there. I must see what it is before we start," said he.

"And I go with you," cried the preacher. "If Judge Lindsly is in danger, my place is by your side. Give me a weapon."

There was no time to parley. Bidding Lawrence stay where he was, Mr. Middleton was helped on one of the horses the Doctor had brought, and the two rode rapidly to the house. They found the servants fleeing through the back door, screaming that Massa Lindsly was being murdered.

The Judge noticed that the Doctor had his revolver in his hand, and called out, "Doctor, don't shoot. This is John Brown, and we are in his power. To resist is instant death."

By this time several of Brown's men were in the room, covering the inmates with their guns.

"Disarm them, see that every one is out of the house, and fire it," said Brown.

"Hold, for the love of God," cried Mr. Middleton. All eyes were turned on him.

"You are John Brown?" he asked of that personage.

"I am," was the answer, "and who are you who call on the name of the Lord?"

"I am the Reverend Arthur Middleton of Ohio. I had a letter of introduction to you, but have lost it."

"I received a letter from an aid society," said Brown, "saying that a Reverend Arthur Middleton was coming. But if you are he, how did you come to be in this nest of the sons of Belial?"

"I fell among thieves," said Mr. Middleton. "This gentleman," pointing to Judge Lindsly, "took me in, bound up my wounds, protected me at the risk of his own life. And this man," pointing to the Doctor, "is the physician who attended me and also helped protect me from the mob. John Brown, I have heard the order you gave to burn this house. Do it, and I will denounce you to the world, to the aid societies; I will make your name a hiss and a byword."

"If all you say is true," said Brown, "I do not understand why I was attacked here. But last night, one William Ketcham and his gang invaded Kansas. By the grace of God, they were driven back, but we have suffered much at the hands of Ketcham and his men, so we followed them up, hoping to take them unawares and wipe them from the face of the earth, but here we ran into a force of armed men. What does it mean?"

"In all probability," answered Mr. Middleton, "you ran into Ketcham and his gang, who came here for the express purpose of lynching me."

"This must be thoroughly looked into," said Brown, "but first we must attend to the wounded. I believe you said this man was a doctor," pointing to Goodnow.

"Yes, and one of God's own noblemen," answered Mr. Middleton.

It was found that only one of Brown's party had been hit, shot through the thigh. He was brought in, and Dr. Goodnow after a short examination, said, "No bones broken, we will soon fix him." And he deftly bound up the wound.

Another wounded man was now brought in, who was groaning bitterly, and seemed to be badly hit, — and what they thought strange,— there was a mask over his face. Doctor Goodnow removed it, and started back in surprise. "Jerry Henshawe, as I live!" he exclaimed.

The man opened his eyes and said, "Oh, Doctor, save me if you can! Why did I ever listen to Ketcham? Why did I ever come here?"

The Doctor examined him carefully. "Jerry, you are bad hit, but you are not going to die. Keep a stiff upper lip; I will pull you through."

Another of Ketcham's men was now brought in

a prisoner. He hung his head in shame, for the prisoner was Dryden, the man who had brought to the Judge the news of the tarring and feathering of Mr. Middleton.

"You are a nice fellow!" said the Doctor. "No wonder you look like a sheep-killing dog. So you thought you would sail under the colors of John Brown. Well, here is the real John Brown, and I reckon you had better be turned over to his tender mercies."

Dryden turned pale. "Don't do that, Doctor," he pleaded.

"Perhaps I can't help myself. Mr. Brown seems to be in command just now."

"Owing to the representations of Mr. Middleton," said Brown, "I shall leave this house and all in it untouched; but I shall have to request the loan of a horse to convey my wounded comrade back to the river. And you?" he said, looking at Mr. Middleton.

"I shall be pleased to go with you," he promptly replied. "It will relieve the Judge of a guest that has caused him both much trouble and danger, and it will save the Doctor that contemplated journey to the river."

"A splendid way out of the difficulty," said the Judge; "but where is the boy?"

"Great Scott! we forgot him," ejaculated the

Doctor. "We left him by the walnut tree. I will go and get him."

"Send a servant," said the Judge. But the Doctor was already away. Soon he returned with Lawrence, who had remained by the tree, although greatly distressed over the absence of his father.

It was arranged that the wounded man was to have one of the horses which the Doctor had brought, and Mr. Middleton the other. "You can turn them loose when you get to the river; that is, if you will," putting a heavy emphasis on the "if you will."

John Brown frowned. "You will get your horses. That is more than I can say of your Missourians who came over into Kansas."

"Look here, John Brown," replied the unabashed Doctor, "You are doing us a good turn to-night by taking this blame preacher who has given us so much trouble, with you. But I don't like you or your methods; and if I ever catch you on Missouri soil again, I will hang you if I can, so help me!"

John Brown smiled grimly. "Do you know," he said, "I have but to say the word, and you will hang now."

"Not while I have this," retorted the Doctor, and quick as thought he whipped out a revolver, and covered Brown. "A move — an order — a sign, and you are a dead man."

Not a sign of fear did Brown show. He looked at the Doctor a moment. "I am not afraid of death, my friend," he replied coolly, "and my death would be but a signal for your own. I like a brave man. Have I not said no one in this house should be harmed? You have simply acted foolishly, not like the brave man you are. Put up your gun."

"Sensible advice," remarked the Doctor, as he put the pistol back in his pocket. "John Brown, I rather like you, blamed if I don't; and now, let me give you a little advice. Be careful, or your fanaticism will hang you some day. You are of the stuff of which martyrs are made."

"As God wills," answered Brown; "but as long as I live my arm will be raised in the cause of the oppressed."

Hurried preparations were now made by Brown for the return to the river. "We have already lingered too long," he said, "and attempt may be made to cut us off."

"Not from here," replied the Judge, "as for us, you go in peace."

Mr. Middleton and Lawrence once more bade good-bye to those who had proven such friends.

"Hurry up," cried the hoarse voice of John Brown, and the little party was swallowed up in the darkness.

"Thank God, they are gone!" exclaimed the Judge.

"And the best way they could have gone, for us," replied the Doctor. "Judge, we are not so popular with our neighbors as we were, but I can't say I am sorry for what we have done. But the Lord save us from any more preachers and from John Brown. Yet it was a fortunate thing for you Brown came."

"When we get things settled," said the Judge, "you and I must have a talk, but let us attend to the dead and wounded first. And, by the way, tell Dryden to stay, I wish to speak to him. Tell him no harm will come to him."

After all had been done for the dead and wounded that could be done, the Judge and the Doctor held a long talk, and then called in Dryden.

"Dryden," said the Judge, "The Doctor and I have agreed that the less talk about this affair the better. Tell Ketcham and the rest of the boys that, as far as we are concerned, nothing will be said of the attempted lynching. The preacher who caused all the trouble is gone. The poor fellow who lies dead here was killed by the Kansas raiders. Your fight here was with them. Let this be known, and those not knowing the full facts will not suspect that you really came to attack my house, and that the meeting with John Brown and his gang was accidental."

"If Ketcham and the rest of the boys do not fall in with that idea, they are fools," answered Dryden.

"Well, that is all, Dryden," said the Judge, "you can go now."

That Ketcham and the boys did fall in with this idea became evident, for before the next day was over, the report was all over the county, of John Brown's raid, and how Ketcham and his party met them at Judge Lindsly's and after a severe fight drove them away, thus saving the Judge's property from destruction. The Judge and the Doctor smiled when they heard the report, but said nothing.

As for Ketcham, there was still fear in his heart, for the preacher had escaped, and the brother of his murdered victim was coming. But why should he let the preacher escape? He could easily follow him to Kansas. The election was the coming week. Kansas would be invaded by hundreds of Missourians. There would be riots, fights, men would be killed. He would make it his business to locate the preacher, and then — he smiled a wicked smile, as he thought of "then."

CHAPTER V

JOHN BROWN and his men lost no time in getting back to the river. Extra precaution had to be taken to guard against surprise. Once they were fired upon from ambush, but without injury. Three hours' hard marching brought them to the river. The ride was a hard one for Mr. Middleton, and the sight of the muddy water of the Missouri was welcome.

As they were about to cross the river, to his surprise he found that George was with them. It will be remembered that George was one of the negroes who went with Lawrence to get his father, and who had spoken of John Brown. He was a very intelligent negro, and had taken a great fancy to Lawrence. When Mr. Middleton discovered his presence, he was filled with dismay. Would Judge Lindsly think he had anything to do with enticing him away? He begged John Brown to send him back with the horses, but Brown was obdurate.

"But you promised Judge Lindsly that nothing should be disturbed on his plantation," urged Mr. Middleton.

"So I did," replied Brown, "and I had nothing to do with this man's coming. He came of his own accord. Never will I be guilty of the great sin of sending a human being back into slavery. I am surprised that you, of all men, should ask it."

So the horses were turned loose, to find their way back, and George accompanied the party. Day was just breaking as they crossed the river. Mr. Middleton turned and looked back over the State where he had suffered so much, and where he had been treated so kindly by those who were naturally his enemies. A bank of clouds lay in the east, and the sun's rays were painting them in all the colors of the rainbow. Soon the whole Missouri side was spread out in all its beauty before him. It was a glorious country. Waving forests, fruitful fields, orchards bending with golden fruit, met his eye. And as he looked, he gave a great sigh. How could so fair a land be cursed with slavery?

He turned his eyes westward. Beyond him, as far as the eye could reach, lay the rolling prairies of Kansas. He could trace the course of murmuring streams, their banks fringed with trees gorgeous in their Autumn dress of red and gold. This was Kansas. This was to be his home. Here was where he was to feed starving souls with the bread of life, and to fight that humanity might be free.

"This is Kansas, my son," said he gently to Lawrence. "Here will we find rest; here will I find work for the Master. Let us kneel down and thank the Lord, that through many dangers at last He has brought us here."

Father and son knelt, and Mr. Middleton poured out his heart in gratitude to God. In mercy, the events of the next few days were hidden from his eyes.

Mr Middleton found a temporary home with a Mr. Harmon, whose claim lay some fifteen miles back from the river. He was received with joy by the settlers; now they could hear the gospel preached. As for George, he could not be induced to leave them. "No," he would say, "I can't leave yo'ng Massa Lawrence; he needs George to look after him." So he stayed, but to Mr. Middleton he was ever a constant reproach. It was through none of his doings that Judge Lindsly had lost his slave. Should he not write to Judge Lindsly, and tell him where George was, so that he could take measures to get him back? It was a fierce battle he fought with conscience. To send a human being back into slavery, or to withhold information from the man who saved his life; these were the questions which racked his soul. He never decided them. It is problematical how he would have decided if he had lived.

As for Ketcham, he was busy with his plans, how to find and make away with Mr. Middleton. He went to consult with his companion in crime, Robert Travers.

"Bob, I believe I have that little killing scrape all fixed," he said, "if we can only find and make away with the preacher."

"I can make away with men in a fight," answered Travers, "but, to tell the truth, I hate this cold-blooded business. What excuse can you make for killing the preacher, if you find him?"

"This: You know Judge Lindsly's nigger George ran away at the time he left. The preacher is a nigger-stealer. How do Missourians serve horse-thieves and nigger-thieves? We have to go over into Kansas on election day, anyway, to show them how to vote. Once locate the preacher, and it's easy. Bob, you were with me in that scrape. You have something at stake, too."

"I know I have; but even if we get the preacher out of the way, how about that brother that's coming?"

"I have thought that all out," answered Ketcham. "I have that letter the brother wrote, name, address, and all. With the preacher out of the way, I will write to Canfield, as a friend of the preacher, saying that before he died, he told me of the case, and requested me to look into it; that I have done so thoroughly, and find that Ketcham has left the country, and can not be located, therefore it would be a waste of time and money for him to come. How is that?"

"Fine, Bill, fine! you have a head on you. I would never have thought of it. I am with you."

"Good! We will put five or six of the other boys on, those we can trust, and we will look after the preacher, while the others do the voting."

"But we must locate him first," urged Travers.

"Sure. And how will Nat White do to send as a spy to find out where he puts up? Nat can pass for a Yankee, any day."

"The very thing. Nat will locate him if any one can."

Nat was found, and willingly accepted the job. Dark clouds were gathering around Mr. Middleton, and death was in the air, but he knew it not.

By election day, there were hundreds of Missourians on Kansas soil. The settlers were driven from the polls in many places, and the ballot boxes stuffed. In some places the Missourians contented themselves by declaring themselves legal voters, and they voted, and voted often. The few settlers saw it would be madness to try to protect themselves, and in most cases they sullenly submitted. There were but few voters in the township in which Mr. Middleton was, and the settlers were in hopes they might escape. A few urged Mr. Middleton to go and vote.

"Why, I have not been in the territory a week!" he exclaimed, astonished that any one should ask him to do such an unlawful act.

One of the men laughed, as he said: "Oh! everybody votes in Kansas; even the cats and dogs are counted."

Mr. Middleton pondered. Evidently the illegal voting was not all on one side, but he firmly refused to have anything to do with it.

George had never seen an election, and decided to go. Thus Mr. Middleton was left alone with the women.

The revolver which Doctor Goodnow had given him when they rushed, as they supposed, to the rescue of Judge Lindsly, the Doctor had bidden him keep, saying that he might find use for it, even in Kansas. But Mr. Middleton thought it ill became a minister to go armed; and when he arrived at Mr. Harmon's was about to lay it away, but Lawrence begged that he might take it and learn to fire it.

"It will do the boy no harm," said Mr. Harmon; and so the father consented, and Lawrence had practised with it four or five times.

It was an anxious day for the women at home. They knew too well what an election day meant in Kansas. But the afternoon came, and so far there had been no alarm, and the settlers began to hope they would escape, when suddenly a company of Missourians swept down upon them. There were so many, it would have been madness to resist. With jest and oath, the Missourians proceeded to empty the ballot box of the votes which were in it and stuff it with their own. Then they gravely counted the ballots, and announced the result as so and so.

When the Missourians were seen coming, George ran in terror; but it was noticed that some half-dozen of the party broke off from the main body and did not stop to interfere with the election, but rode straight on. They soon overtook George; and the leader, who was Ketcham, yelled: "Boys, we are in luck. There is Judge Lindsly's nigger that the preacher run off with. A nice little sum we will get for taking him back." Giving George in charge of one of the men, he exclaimed: "Boys, we have the nigger; now for the nigger-thief. We will give him a taste of Missouri justice." And with a whoop and hurrah they galloped on.

Well had Nat White, Ketcham's spy, done his duty. Ketcham knew just where to find Mr. Middleton. Before they reached the sod abode of Mr. Harmon, they made a detour around, so as to come up in the rear.

It was a complete surprise. Mr. Middleton was out in the yard, and he was in the hands of his enemies before he could raise a finger to resist.

The women began to scream, but they were told to shut up, or the house would be burned over their heads.

"Come, boys, some one bring a rope!" shouted Ketcham. "Let 's do this work quick. Here is a good place," pointing to a pole which projected from the roof of the stable.

The rope was brought, and thrown over the head of their victim, and they were on the point of dragging him to the place of execution, when one of their number gave a startled cry. Looking up, they saw John Brown at the head of half a dozen men, bearing down on them.

"The sword of the Lord and of Gideon!" shouted Brown, as he flourished an old sabre above his head, and came down on them like a thunderbolt.

With yells of terror, the Missourians sprang for their horses, and with whip and spur urged them to their highest speed.

Ketcham lingered a moment too long. "Hell and furies! you shall not escape," he yelled; and snatching a pistol from his belt, he pressed the muzzle against the breast of Mr. Middleton, fired, and turned to flee. But as he turned there was a report of another pistol, and he fell doubled up in a heap.

The smoking revolver dropped from the hand of Lawrence, for it was he who fired the shot, and with a cry of anguish, he flung himself on the body of his father. To him the dead raider was nothing. He hardly realized what he had done. He only felt that his father was dead or dying.

"Father! Father! speak to me," he cried in piteous accents. "It's I; it's Lawrence."

The dying man opened his eyes, saw Lawrence

As he turned there was a report of another pistol

bending over him, smiled, and feebly raised his arms as if to embrace him. The blood was welling up from a great wound in the breast.

Kind hands picked him up, carried him into the house, and placed him on a bed. They tried to examine the wound; but he whispered, " No, you can do no good. I have but a short time to live. Leave me alone with my son. I must speak to him before I die. I have that which I must say to him."

Softly, and with bowed heads, all went out, and left father and son alone.

CHAPTER VI

THE DYING REQUEST

"MY poor boy," faintly said Mr. Middleton, "listen closely to what I have to say, for soon you will have no father."

"You must not die; I cannot let you die; if you die I want to die, too," cried the boy in an agony of grief, and it seemed as if his sobs would choke him.

"Lawrence, control yourself. If not, I shall pass away before I say to you what I wish."

With a great effort, Lawrence held back his sobs. "Now, father, I can listen," he whispered.

"First, let us thank God, my son, that He is permitting me to die as I shall, and not the ignominious death of a felon."

"Ketcham will never try to hang another man," said Lawrence.

"Why, did Brown kill him?" asked Mr. Middleton.

"No, I shot him, just after he shot you."

The father shuddered. His son so young, and the blood of a fellow creature on his hands! But he felt his strength going, and what he had to say he must say at once. His speech was so broken, and he had to stop so often that we will write in connected form, what he had to say.

"Lawrence, after I am gone, the only near relative that you will have is my brother Alfred, who resides in St. Louis. Your mother was an orphan when I married her, and she had no brother or sister. In my own family there were only us two, Alfred and I. He was four years older than I, and I looked upon him as my protector. No two brothers ever loved one another more.

" He was bold and aggressive; I, rather timid. I was of a religious nature; he did not give much thought to religious subjects, but he was the soul of honor. Like so many others, he believed the West furnished better opportunities for advancement than the East and decided to try his fortune there. He finally settled in St. Louis, and was very successful in business. There he married a rich Southern lady, who owned two or three plantations with a large number of slaves.

"I remained in Ohio, took a college course, and, as you know, became a minister. My life was a very happy one until your mother died. But I had you, and in you I found comfort. I always hated slavery and am what is known as an Abolitionist. When my brother became a slaveowner, I wrote him a sharp letter which he answered good-naturedly, saying, if I knew more about slavery, I would think better of it.

"Just before you were born, I visited him. While there, he sold a negro who had become unruly, to a trader to be taken South. The negro had a wife and child, and when I witnessed their parting, I became very indignant, and expressed myself strongly.

"'Oh, pshaw!' he replied, laughingly, 'she will forget him in a week, and have another man.'

"The heartlessness of the remark angered me, and in my rage I said something which he said reflected on his wife. He in turn became very angry, ordered me from the house, and said he never wanted to see or hear from me again. And thus we parted, rage in the heart of each. I have never seen him or heard directly from him since; but I understand he is now a banker, and considered one of the wealthiest men in the city.

"I now see I was more to blame than he. I have learned that a man can own slaves, and yet be a good man, like Judge Lindsly. I have also learned that our moral and religious opinions are largely the result of our education and environments. If I had been born in the South, I might have had a very different opinion of slavery.

"Lawrence, when I am gone, I want you to go to my brother. I want you to tell him that while I still believe that slavery is one of the greatest curses of the age, that I was wrong in saying what I did of those who own slaves. His wife, your Aunt Clara, is one of the sweetest women I ever met.

God forgive me for wronging her in what I said. Tell them to forgive me; that I will rest easier if they do. You will go to them and tell them this, will you not, Lawrence?"

"Yes, father, but I cannot believe you did anything wrong," replied the boy brokenly.

His father's last words were very broken, and Lawrence had hard work to put them together connectedly.

After Lawrence had promised, his father whispered: "Kiss me, Lawrence."

Lawrence pressed a kiss on his forehead. It was already damp with the dew of death.

"Lawrence — boy, it's growing dark; hold my hand."

Lawrence took the hand, his tears raining down upon it. His father's lips moved; and bending over, Lawrence heard the whispered words:

"The Lord is my shepherd, I shall not want. He maketh me to lie down in green pastures; he leadeth me beside the still waters.

"Yea, though I walk through the valley of the shadow of death, I will fear no evil; for thou art with me; thy rod and thy staff they comfort me."

A smile as of heavenly peace came over the face of the dying man and he lay very still. Through his blinding tears, Lawrence did not see, but the hand he held grew strangely chill. Then he noticed, and a cry of agony broke from his lips.

Those who had waited in silence outside, that father and son might be alone, came in. Kind hands led the weeping boy away. As a mother comforts her child, so did Mrs. Harmon comfort the fatherless boy, and with his head pillowed on her sympathetic breast, after a while he sobbed himself to sleep.

John Brown came in and looked on the face of the dead, and as he looked, his eyes gleamed with a fanatical fire, and his hands were clenched tightly.

"Would we had come a few minutes earlier," he said, "and not one of the sons of Belial would have escaped. But the Lord be praised! The vengeance of the Almighty has been swift and sure on the murderer."

Before he left — for Brown was on his way to a more southern point in the Territory — he gave Lawrence his blessing, and kissing him, said, "My son, through all your life, love God, and hate slavery."

These were his last words to Lawrence, who was never to see him again. In after years, when the name of John Brown had become a household word, Lawrence wished he had been older, that he might have studied the real character of that remarkable man. As it was, it seemed to him he was a combination of the tenderest love, and the fiercest hate; that his religious zeal amounted to fanaticism; and that he was ready at all times, and in all places, to smite the enemies of the Lord. But older heads than Lawrence's have analyzed Brown's character, and the disagreement is so great, the world is none the wiser.

Never did that thinly settled country see a greater funeral than that which gathered to pay the last respects to the remains of the Reverend Arthur Middleton. The people came from miles around. He had been with them scarcely a week, but his sad story flew, as it were, on the wings of the wind.

Loving hands made his coffin; the loving and tender hands of women prepared his shroud. He was laid to rest amid the tears of what was, for that country, a vast concourse. He was buried on a knoll which overlooked the country for miles around, and which had already been consecrated by the settlers as the last resting-place of their few dead.

Many were the words of love and sympathy spoken to the orphan boy. Women wept over him, as if his sorrow were their own. Not a house for miles around but would gladly have opened its doors to him. Most of them were rude and poor, but in them were kind and loving hearts. More than one mother would have taken the lonely boy to her bosom as one of her own children.

You boys and girls who reside in great cities, you can little understand the tenderness and love which exist in the country when death comes. In the city you are lost, and no one heeds when affliction comes; but in the country, especially a new country, it is different. There, the human heart, untrammelled by the lust for wealth, and unfettered from selfish ambition, knows and feels for the sorrow of others.

Mr. and Mrs. Harmon pressed Lawrence to make their home his home, to be as one of their own children. But when he told them of his father's last wishes, and of his promise to obey them, they said no more. The request of the dead should be heeded, but it was with sad hearts they consented to give him up.

Of the money which had been sewed in Lawrence's clothes, there was over a hundred dollars left. The kind settlers would not take a cent. There were no funeral expenses.

Mr. Harmon proved a wise adviser. "I will go with you to Leavenworth," he said. "You must have a good outfit of clothes. From what your father said, your uncle must be very rich, and you must go looking respectable. After the clothes are bought, there will be enough left to secure cabin passage. You must travel like the little gentleman that you are."

At last all preparations were completed, and Lawrence was ready to start. The last thing he did was to visit his father's grave. He threw himself down on the earth and bedewed it with burning tears. It seemed to him that it was his father, not his lifeless remains, that he was leaving; and, oh! it was so cruel to leave him there to sleep all alone — leave him for the rain to beat down upon his grave, the cold snows of winter to cover it.

His faith was weak; his heart, crushed with grief, could not look beyond the grave. It was there his father was. The last rays of the setting sun were touching the mound, as he knelt to say the last farewell. All around the prairie was brown and sere; the touch of Autumn and of death was on the earth; but in the west the sun was setting in a blaze of glory. Was this glory the harbinger of what was beyond?

CHAPTER VII

DOWN THE RIVER

WITH the first light of day, Mr. Harmon and Lawrence started for Leavenworth. His parting with Mrs. Harmon caused his tears to flow afresh, and the good woman clung to him, as if she could not let him go. She kissed him again and again, and called him her darling boy. But the last good-bye had to be said, and they were on their way.

For the first few miles, Lawrence said little. His heart was like lead, and he felt that when he parted with Mr. Harmon, he would part with the last friend he had on earth. He dreaded to meet his uncle, the man who had quarrelled with his father. What kind of a reception would he have? Mr. Harmon respected his silence, and said little. Thus mile after mile was passed. The country through which they were journeying was a beautiful one. On every side stretched the broad prairies, now brown and sere, under the Autumn sky. Here and there could be seen the humble abode of some settler; and two or three times they passed the charred remains of some cabin. The Missouri border ruffians had come that way.

But childhood is ever buoyant and hopeful, and

sorrow cannot forever bind it. Almost before Lawrence realized it, he was talking with Mr. Harmon, asking him questions, and seeking his advice. He could not have had a better adviser.

Mr. Harmon was a well read, educated man. He had been a school teacher in the East, but like so many others, he had come to Kansas to help to make it free, and to carve out for himself a home. Little by little he drew from Lawrence all that his father had told him. He looked grave when told of the quarrel the brothers had had, and that there had been no intercourse between them for twelve years.

"Lawrence, you must be careful," he said; "let me give you some advice. I gather from what you say, that your uncle is very wealthy; that he is a slaveholder, and firmly wedded to the belief that slavery is right. Your father and he quarrelled bitterly on the subject, and parted in anger. When he learns that your father lost his life in trying to make Kansas free, it will not add to your welcome.

"Yet, your father says he is a good man, and that he himself was more to blame than his brother, for in the heat of the argument he said what should not have been said. Now do not make the same mistake that your father made. Whatever your feelings on the question of slavery are — and I well know what they are — keep silent. Never argue the question of the right or wrong of slavery while under his roof. Young as you are, they will not expect you to be a partisan, one way or the other. You understand what I mean, do you not?"

"Yes," answered the boy. "I am not to lie, and pretend to be what I am not; but I am to accept the situation in my uncle's household, and find no fault. If I see things I don't like, I am to keep still. Above all, I am never to tell uncle it is wrong to keep slaves."

"That is it, Lawrence," said Mr. Harmon, much gratified. "You understand perfectly, and are wise beyond your years."

Lawrence was soon to learn how valuable the advice was which Mr. Harmon gave him.

In due time Leavenworth was reached, and they learned that a steamboat was due from the north that evening, and would not leave until the next morning.

"First," said Mr. Harmon, "we will go to the office of the steamboat line, and secure your ticket. We shall then know how much money you will have left for clothes. You must also keep some. When travelling, there is no friend like money."

They found that a ticket for cabin passage would make quite a hole in Lawrence's slender means. The agent advised him to secure a ticket at once, as the boat would be crowded. This advice Mr. Harmon confirmed.

When Lawrence handed the agent the money to pay for the ticket, that functionary scrutinized the bills very carefully, looked over some papers, and then said: "I am sorry, my boy, but I cannot take this money. Most of it is worthless; what is not is subject to a heavy discount."

Had a bolt of lightning fallen from a clear sky, they would not have been more astonished. Lawrence staggered as if struck. What did it mean?

"Here," continued the agent, holding up a twenty-dollar bill, "is a bill that two days ago I would have considered good. Yesterday we heard that the bank had gone down. Hundreds of banks are failing all over the country, and paper money is becoming almost valueless."

Lawrence gazed at Mr. Harmon in mute appeal, then burst into tears, and sank into a chair, completely overcome. As for Mr. Harmon, he was as greatly distressed as Lawrence; but he tried to cheer the boy up by saying: "Never mind, Lawrence. You will have to go back with me, and be my boy, after all."

"Let me see the rest of your money," said the agent, kindly.

Lawrence handed him all he had. The agent looked it over carefully, and then said: "Here is a bill I can take, but there is a heavy discount on it. Let's see,"— and he figured a while,— "there will be just about enough to pay deck passage to St. Louis. It's the best I can do, but it will be a rough passage for such a little fellow as you."

Mr. Harmon urged Lawrence to return with him, but the boy stoutly refused.

"No, I promised father to go to St. Louis, and I will go, if I have to walk," Lawrence replied firmly.

Mr. Harmon saw that it was useless to urge him further, so a ticket for deck passage was bought, but it left the boy penniless. When he left Mr. Harmon's his few belongings had been placed in an old carpet bag, as he had expected to buy a neat trunk at Leavenworth. Out of his own slender purse Mr. Harmon now purchased a goodly supply of bread and meat, carefully wrapped in paper, and the packages were placed in the carpet bag. It was all the provisions that Lawrence would have until he reached St. Louis. Deck passengers had to feed themselves.

The parting with Mr. Harmon was a painful one. With him gone, Lawrence would be alone, among strangers, and penniless. But he choked back his sobs, as he bade Mr. Harmon farewell, and cautioned him to tell Mrs. Harmon that he was all right.

But Mr. Harmon afterwards confessed that he had never seen his wife so angry as when he arrived at home and told how he had left the boy. "Why," he exclaimed, "she would hardly speak to me for a week."

It was after dark before the boat drew up at the

dock at Leavenworth. Lawrence started to go on board, but the boat was unloading and taking freight, and he was pushed and jostled and cursed, and told to get out of the way. The mate was swearing lustily at the roustabouts, and Lawrence shuddered at the language he used. But he was to become accustomed to it before reaching St. Louis.

As the boat was to lie at Leavenworth all night, the passengers from that place were not expected to come on board until morning, but Lawrence had no place to go, so he stood aside, and watched the loading and unloading. At last the din and hustle ceased, the crowd on the dock dispersed, and the gang plank was about to be hauled in, when Lawrence darted across it onto the boat.

"Here, you little rascal, where are you going?" cried an officer, catching him by the collar. "You get out of this."

"Please, sir, I have a ticket," said Lawrence.

"A ticket? Let's see it," gruffly replied the official.

Lawrence handed him his ticket. He glanced at it and then said, "Why did n't you wait until morning?"

"Please, sir, I had nowhere else to go," answered Lawrence.

"Well, get out of the way; roost on a box, if you want to, but don't let me find you sneaking around," and he gave the boy a push, and sent him in among the bales and boxes.

At a loss where to go or what to do, he sat on a box looking around, and wondering where he would sleep. He noticed that in a place where the deck was bare of merchandise, a number of men were lying asleep, some with blankets over them, others with their heads on dirty bundles, and no covering.

At last, mustering up courage, he asked a petty officer who seemed to have charge of the deck (for he had seen him go along, and stir up two or three of the sleeping men with his foot, and tell them to move along, and not block up the passage) where he could sleep, as he would like to go to bed.

The man looked at him in surprise, and burst into a hearty laugh. "Why, sonny, do you expect this 'ere boat to furnish feather-beds and state-rooms for deck passengers?"

Seeing the distressed look on Lawrence's face, the man asked, "Whar air you goin', sonny?"

"To St. Louis," answered Lawrence faintly.

"An' all alone? Whar is your father?"

"He is dead, sir. I am going to an uncle in St. Louis," said Lawrence, holding back a sob. "I thought I had money enough to buy cabin passage, but the agent said it was bad — bank just broke."

"Blast the banks!" exclaimed the man; "lost twenty-five dollars myself. I will see what I can do for you, sonny."

The man looked around and found a bale of goods

squeezed in between two large boxes. There was just room between the two boxes for Lawrence to get in.

" There," said the man, " you crawl in there, an' you will have one of the nicest beds the deck affords."

Lawrence did as he was bid, and being very tired he was soon fast asleep, and did not awake until the noise and confusion aroused him early the next morning. Bewildered, he looked around, and at first did not realize where he was, then recollection came, and he crawled out of his narrow quarters.

Already the deck hands were eating their coarse breakfast. Lawrence opened his carpet sack, and ate heartily of his bread and meat. Then placing the sack in the place where he had slept, he began to look around. All was bustle and confusion, as on the night before. More freight was taken on, passengers came streaming on board, and the boat was soon under way. But it had not gone far before it stuck on a sand bar, and there it remained until afternoon.

Boy-like, he grew tired and restless, and began to wander around and, at last, found his way into the cabin. How nice it was! What a fine time he could have had, if only he could have taken cabin passage.

Just then the first mate came through the cabin

and noticed him. "Here, you boy," he exclaimed, "what are you doing here? Have you a cabin ticket?"

"No, sir," said Lawrence, "only a deck ticket."

"Then get down whar you belong, an' don't let me see you up heah agin," and the officer gave him a box on the ear which set him rolling.

Lawrence arose, his ear tingling, and his face aflame with passion. "If I were a man, I would whip you," he cried.

For a moment the mate stood astonished, and then burst into a coarse laugh. "I like your spunk, my little rooster," he said, "but it takes a man to whip me. Now you git."

But the blow had been seen by several of the passengers, and among them, by a dainty little miss not more than eight years of age. Shaking her tiny fist at the mate, and stamping her foot, she said:

"You bad, bad man, to strike a little boy! You ought to be 'shamed of yourself."

The mate turned very red in the face, and walked away.

"Lola, what are you doing?" cried a sharp voice. "Come here this minute!"

But it seemed that the little miss had not been in the habit of obeying very promptly, for instead of going to her mother, she called out, "Mamma, the big man struck the little boy"; and going up to

Lawrence, she said, "Little boy, did it hurted you? Lola is sorry."

But by this time her mother had her by the arm, dragging her away, and Lawrence was beating a hasty retreat. The cabin saw no more of him during the passage, but he often thought of the little girl, and wondered if her mother punished her.

It was so late when the boat arrived at Kansas City that it tied up for the night, and Lawrence once more crept into the space between the boxes and slept. In the morning when he went to get his carpet sack for some breakfast, it was nowhere to be found. Some one had stolen it during the night. Stunned by this second blow of misfortune, he sat down utterly disconsolate. "I might as well die, and be done with it," he thought.

The man who was watch on the deck, the one who had showed him the place in which to sleep, noticed him, and said, "What now, my little fellow? What's wrong this morning?"

Lawrence told him of his new trouble.

"Well, you are in hard luck. Reckon, though, if you don't say anything I can fix you."

The deck hands were already eating their breakfast, and the kind-hearted watchman went and spoke to the cook. Soon a tin cup of black coffee and some black bread was given to Lawrence; and during the rest of the trip down the river, the deck hands saw that Lawrence did not lack for food such as it was. There is kindness in the human heart, even among the ignorant and degraded.

At Kansas City, a gang of half a dozen negroes, handcuffed together, was brought on board by a negro-trader. While Lawrence was pitying their forlorn condition, to his astonishment he saw that one of them was George. His face bore a look of utter dejection. Watching his chance, when no one was near, Lawrence went up, and spoke to him. George's face lighted up when he saw who it was.

Lawrence learned that Travers, who had taken command of the Missourians after the death of Ketcham, instead of taking him back to his master, had sold him to a trader to be taken down the river.

" Oh! Massa Lawrence," he groaned, " it was a bad day for me when I run away from Massa Lindsly. Now, I go 'way down South."

"I am sorry, George," said Lawrence. "You should have minded father, and gone back."

Here the conversation was stopped by the trader who came to see how his charges were getting along. He swore roundly at Lawrence and told him if he ever found him talking with his niggers again he would break his neck. After this Lawrence took notice, and saw that no one, not even the deck hands, spoke to the poor fellows. They were left alone in their misery.

At every place the boat stopped going down the river, there was great rejoicing over the result of the recent election. Buchanan had been triumphantly elected, and the South was happy. In many places where the boat stopped, bonfires were blazing, and the people were holding a jubilee.

One day Lawrence overheard the trader talking to a gentleman whom he had brought down to see his niggers. "They air a likely lot," said the trader, "an' I bought them dirt-cheap. You see, some of them upper-river fellers got scared thinkin' Frémont might be elected; but now ole Buck got in, niggers will go up."

"Do you think Buchanan will be as favorable to the South as Pierce?" asked the gentleman.

"Suah, he is all right," was the answer.

"I am almost sorry that Frémont was not elected," said the gentleman.

The trader opened his eyes in astonishment.

"What's that you say?" he asked. "It's not possible you have turned Abolitionist?"

The gentleman laughed. "Not yet, Evans," he answered. "But if Frémont had been elected, it would have given the South an excuse to secede from the Union. I am sick and tired of being yoked up with the Northern Abolitionists. The South will never come to her own until she is a separate Government."

"Right you air, Colonel. And we are blamed fools for not bustin' the Union long ago."

"It's coming, Evans, it's coming, and that before

long. Let's go and take a drink to the coming Southern Republic." And the two adjourned to the bar.

The voyage down the stream was a long one. The water in the river was low, and the steamer stuck several times. The passengers grumbled, and the captain swore, but that did not raise the river.

At any time a journey down the Missouri is a monotonous one. There is nothing pretty about the Missouri. It runs between low clay banks, that are continually being eaten away. Its channel is shifting, and where the water is deep one day, may be a sand bar the next. The pilot can guide his boat only by the looks of the water; charts are no good. Although one of the longest of rivers, it is one of the meanest to navigate, and since the day of railroads, navigation has almost ceased. But at the time of which we write, it was the great artery of commerce between St. Louis and the West.

Lawrence noticed that the little girl who had befriended him got off the boat at Jefferson City. He felt more lonely than ever, even though he had not seen her since the day he invaded the cabin.

Before the voyage was over, Lawrence was a sight to behold. Having no change of clothing, he was covered with the smoke and grime of the boat, and he became so dirty he loathed himself. How could he present himself to his uncle in this condition? What would they think of him? The thought troubled him, and before he reached St. Louis he became haunted with the fear that his uncle would not receive him.

But all things must come to an end, and at last the steamer drew up to the wharf at St. Louis. The voyage was over.

CHAPTER VIII

MR. ALFRED MIDDLETON

IT was a dirty, scared, and faint-hearted boy that stepped from the steamboat, and not until most of the other passengers had gone, did Lawrence muster up courage to go ashore. The more he thought of meeting his uncle, the more he dreaded it.

The noise and confusion of the great dock appalled him, and it looked to him as if all the steamboats in the world had gathered at St. Louis. He had tried to scrub his face and hands before he left the boat, but they were almost as grimy as ever. He had no idea where to go, or of whom to inquire about his uncle.

As he stood undecided what to do, a crowd of wharf hoodlums swooped down upon him.

"Hi! sonny, whar you goin'? an' whar you come from?" they shouted.

Lawrence looked at them disdainfully, and without saying a word, tried to push past them.

"Pards, he is a 'ristocrat, he won't notice we'uns," cried one who appeared to be the leader. "Jes' look at his clo'es. My! but arn't they swell? Most as good as we'uns. Le's 'nitiate him, pards," and they made for him.

Lawrence defended himself gallantly, but there

were too many of them, and he was getting the worst of it, when one of them cried, "Hi! boys, heah comes a cop," and they scattered in every direction.

Lawrence came out of the *mêlée* in a dilapidated condition. His hat was gone, his face was bloody, and his coat was torn in tatters.

The policeman came up, and roughly seizing him by the shoulder said, "Phat do ye mane by foightin' here? Oi will have to run yez in."

"Please, sir," said Lawrence, "I couldn't help it. I just got off the steamboat when all those boys pitched onto me."

"Jist got off the boat, did ye? Where ye goin'? An' where ye come from?"

"I came from Leavenworth, Kansas, sir, and I am trying to find my uncle. Perhaps you know him."

"An' who may yer uncle be?" asked the policeman.

"Mr. Alfred Middleton, sir."

"Howly Virgin! Alfred Middleton yer uncle! The gintleman will be glad to see his nephew, no doubt. Why did n't he sind his kerrige for ye?" And the policeman shook with laughter.

"He is my uncle, all the same," cried Lawrence, for he saw the policeman did not believe him, "and I want to find him."

"Well, sonny, go find him. Oi will let ye go this time, but if Oi ketch ye here agin, Oi will run ye in. Do ye hear?"

"Yes, sir," said Lawrence meekly, as he made off.

The policeman looked puzzled. "Queer kid that," he said. "He don't talk like a street gamin; but Alfred Middleton his uncle!" And the policeman went off into a fit of laughter again.

Lawrence lost no time in escaping. His first stop was at a public fountain where he washed the blood from his face. He had been told to ask a policeman where his uncle lived, but now he dare not ask one; he would surely be " run in," so he kept on going up the street he was on.

At last he mustered up courage, and asked a genteel looking man if he knew where Mr. Alfred Middleton lived. The man stared at him, and passed on without answering. He asked others; they looked at him, laughed, and went on. Utterly discouraged, he at last sat down on the curb, and sobbed as if his heart would break. Hundreds passed by, looked at him curiously, and hurried on.

"What 's the matter, little boy? What can I do for you?" said a friendly voice.

Lawrence looked up and saw a rather short man, dressed quite plainly, standing by him.

"What is it?" again asked the gentleman. "Have some of the other boys stolen your papers, and beaten you for crying out?"

The kind face of the man at once won the confidence of Lawrence. "I had no papers to sell," he answered, "but I want to find my uncle."

"Your uncle, and who may he be?"

"Mr. Alfred Middleton, sir."

The gentleman started. "Alfred Middleton your uncle? I know him by reputation; but this is strange."

"Oh! sir, can you tell me where he lives?"

"Yes; but if Alfred Middleton is your uncle, how came you here in such a condition?"

Lawrence told his story, and the gentleman listened attentively.

"It may be true what you say, I don't know; but if not true, there will be little harm done."

Thus saying he signalled a passing street car. It stopped, and the gentleman spoke a few words to the conductor, and handed him five cents.

"All right, Captain," said the conductor, "but I reckon you are bitten. Jump aboard!" This to Lawrence.

"Who is that gentleman?" asked Lawrence as he climbed aboard, and the car started.

"That, you little rascal, is Captain Grant," answered the conductor, scowling at him. "So you worked him for a street-car fare, did you? You the nephew of Alfred Middleton? What a little liar you must be!"

"I am no liar," replied Lawrence. "Mr. Middleton is my uncle."

"All right, have it your own way, but if you go there, and don't get kicked down the steps, I am mistaken," growled the conductor, as he hustled forward to collect fares.

The car was soon in the most aristocratic residence portion of the city. It stopped, and the conductor said to Lawrence, pointing down the cross street: "Mr. Middleton lives down that street a block or two. Now get out quick."

The conductor chuckled when he started the car. "I would like to see his reception," he said to himself. "He Alfred Middleton's nephew! This will be a good one to tell the boys."

Lawrence went slowly down the street, reading the names on the door-plates. Each step that he took, it seemed harder to take the next. He was trembling all over. More than once he thought he must run away. He had read about boys in great cities making a living by selling papers. Captain Grant had taken him for a newsboy. Why could he not sell papers? Then he thought of his promise to his father, and mustering all his courage, he went on.

Soon he came to a mansion, grander and more imposing, he thought, than its neighbors, and on the door-plate he read the name, "Alfred Middleton." Lawrence's heart was in his mouth. How could he ever ascend those marble steps, and demand admittance to that magnificent palace? Mustering all his courage, he went up the steps, halting on every one. At last the door was reached, and with trembling hand, he rang the bell.

The door was opened by a negro who by his manner might have been taken for the proprietor of the house. His eye fell on Lawrence.

"Did you ring dat door bell?" he asked angrily.

"Yes, sir, I —"

"You git, or I give you to de perlice," and the door was slammed in his face.

Lawrence had been given no opportunity of explaining who he was. He must try again. He must have it out with that pompous negro, and once more he rang the bell.

Again the door opened. "You heah yet?" now cried the thoroughly angry servant. "I'll larn you," and he drew back his foot to kick Lawrence off the steps.

Lawrence saw the movement. "Touch me if you dare!" he cried. "Mr. Middleton is my uncle."

The butler, for such he was, stared in openmouthed astonishment. This ragged, dirty street Arab, the nephew of Mr. Middleton? Impossible!

"You lyin' dirty white-trash, you git," and again he drew back his foot to kick him.

"You touch me, and your back will smart," cried Lawrence, his timidity all gone. He had learned while at Judge Lindsly's that a slave could not commit a more heinous crime than to strike a white person.

The butler stood aghast. Who was this ragged boy who thus dared to defy him?

Just then a fine carriage drawn by a span of prancing black horses drew up at the door. A black coachman in immaculate livery held the reins, and a footman stood on the step behind. As the carriage stopped, the footman sprang lightly to the ground. He took in the little comedy at the door with a broad grin, and taking off his hat, he bowed in mock servility to the butler.

"What's de mattah, William?" he asked. "Yo' Majesty pears to be flabbergasted."

"Dis, dis white-trash," said the butler pointing to Lawrence in disgust, "says dat Massa Middleton is his uncle."

"Golly!" he shouted, "what a —"

But he stopped short, and stood respectfully at attention, hat in hand. A lady, wrapped for a ride, had stepped out of the door. She looked with questioning eyes, first at Lawrence, and then at the servants.

"What does all this mean?" she asked coldly, "and who is this ragged boy?"

"Missy Middleton," replied the butler volubly, "dis boy, he rang de doah-bell, and when I threaten him wid de perlice, he say," and his voice sank to a whisper, "he say Massa Middleton is his uncle."

The lady turned to Lawrence, and asked sternly, "What do you mean by such a story? William, call the police."

"Just one moment, lady!" cried Lawrence trem-

bling at the thought of the police. " Mr. Middleton
is really and truly my uncle. I am his brother
Arthur's son."

" Hold, William," commanded the lady, for the
butler had turned to go. " This must be looked into.
Mr. Middleton has a brother Arthur."

Then turning to Lawrence, she asked, " Where is
your father ? "

" He is dead," answered Lawrence with a sob.

" Strange," murmured the lady. " Alfred has
not heard from his brother for years. I remember
they parted in anger. Can it be possible this disreputable looking boy is his brother's son ? "

She knitted her brow as in thought, and then turning to the august butler said: " William, take this
boy to the servants' quarters. Mind, answer no
questions, and let as few see him as possible. I was
just going to drive to the bank for Mr. Middleton.
I will bring him as quickly as possible. Keep the
boy until we come."

Saying this, she entered the carriage, and was
driven rapidly away.

" Come," said the butler surlily to Lawrence, " an'
mind you don't speak to any one, an' don't you brush
'gainst anything wid 'em dirty clo'es."

Thus reminded, Lawrence was conducted to the
servants' quarters, the butler haughtily refusing to
answer a question. He showed Lawrence into a
small room, and left him with the parting injunction :

"Mind now, don't you stir till Massa Middleton sends for you!"

In the meantime, Mrs. Middleton was being driven to the bank, much perturbed in spirit. Could it be possible this boy was really her husband's nephew? And if he was, what was to be done? She shivered at the thought.

As Mr. Middleton entered the carriage he said: "Clara, don't you want to take a little spin through the park before you go home? This is one of the few remaining days of the year we can enjoy it."

"No, Alfred," was the answer, "we had better get home as soon as possible. A very strange thing happened just as I started." And then she told him of what had occurred. To say that Mr. Middleton was astonished, is to express it mildly.

"What kind of looking boy was he?" he asked.

"As dirty and disreputable-looking a specimen as I ever saw on the street, and he had all the appearance of having been in a fight. There was blood on his clothes, and I noticed his nose was a little swollen, and come to think about it, he had no hat."

Mr. Middleton shrugged his shoulders. "An impostor likely," he remarked. "Some of these street gamins are wonderfully cunning."

"I don't know," answered his wife. "So I thought at first, but there was something about the boy I could not understand. He bore himself proudly, not cringingly, as usual with such boys, and his language was good."

"And did you say that he told you that his father was dead?" Mr. Middleton's voice faltered a little as he asked the question.

"Yes, and there were tears in his voice as he told me."

"Strange! Strange!" said Mr. Middleton as if to himself, and then, "Clara, you remember my brother Arthur, don't you?"

"Yes, perfectly. He was very much of a gentleman, and finely educated. A professor in some college, was he not?"

"Yes, but a fanatic on the subject of slavery. That is what we quarrelled about. When he as much as said you and I would go straight to hell if we did not free our slaves, and intimated that no refined Christian woman would own slaves, it was more than I could stand. That was reflecting on you, dearest."

"What if this waif should really prove to be his son?" she queried.

"We shall see. It would not do to let him starve; but to acknowledge him as my nephew! It makes me shiver to think of it."

"We could quietly get him a home some place, and not let it be known that he was your nephew," she replied timidly.

"Yes, but the chances are the boy is an impostor. Don't let us worry until we know."

But that the stately Mr. Middleton was ill at ease his wife could plainly see. "Drive fast," was his order to the coachman, and they were soon at home.

"How about that boy, William?" he asked of the butler as soon as he entered the house. Whereupon with many embellishments, William told of his encounter with Lawrence.

"Go and bring him to me at once — in the library," ordered the master.

"Pardon, massa," said William, "but dat boy is jes' too dirty to bring anywhar. I put him in dat little room we keep rubbish in. He will dirty eben dat."

"Very well, William, I will see him there. It's better, for, if he should prove an impostor, the police can take him out the back way."

From what his wife and William had said, Mr. Middleton was prepared to see a very disreputable specimen of the street gamin; but he was not quite prepared to see what he did.

Lawrence was dejectedly sitting on a box. His rags hung around him in strings, and he looked as if the grime of a coal mine had been ground into his clothes. His tear-stained face was streaked with black, for he had tried to wipe away his tears with his sleeve.

"Great heavens!" thought Mr. Middleton, "can this boy be my nephew?"

"Massa Middleton, sah," said William.

Lawrence sprang to his feet, and drew himself proudly up. He saw before him a man about fifty years of age, with slightly gray hair, and with eyes which seemed to look him through and through. His mouth and chin denoted firmness and decision of character. Yet it was not an unpleasant face. Mr. Middleton was called a very handsome man. Lawrence saw that he bore a resemblance to his father, but he was a much larger man, and his face was not so refined. He looked more like a man of the world than the boy's dead father.

"Your nephew, sir," said Lawrence, not boastingly, but as a matter of fact.

It was not the greeting that Mr. Middleton expected. It rather surprised him; but collecting himself, he replied curtly, "That remains to be seen."

He now put Lawrence through an examination that would have done honor to a lawyer. But Lawrence proved a star witness. He was well informed on the history of his father's family, and answered every question correctly, and without hesitation.

Mr. Middleton bit his lip in vexation. This boy was no doubt his nephew. What should he do with him? That he would decide later, but one thing was certain, he must be cleaned up.

"How was it you came to me?" he asked.

"Because my dying father requested it," answered Lawrence.

"But your condition, how did that come? Surely your father did not live in filth and rags."

"It is a long, a horrible story, sir, but poor father is not to blame for my condition."

"Never mind now, if the story is long and as you say, a horrible one," said Mr. Middleton, "I can hear it after a while. The first thing is to make you look a little more decent. I can then listen to your story with much better grace."

Then turning to his butler he said: "We have no time to get a tailor-made suit for this boy. Take his measure, and go to a clothing store, and buy a suit. The best they have. Buy everything, underclothing, hat, shoes, you understand."

"Yes, massa, I understand."

"One thing more. Before you go, conduct my — this boy to the bathroom, and let him thoroughly cleanse himself, by the time you get back with the clothes."

"Yes, sah," said the butler.

But when he was out of his master's sight he sniffed contemptuously, and with head high in air, led the way to the bathroom.

As Mr. Middleton joined his wife, she looked at him inquiringly. "He is Arthur's boy, all right," he said. "I never saw a worse-looking little vagabond, but he is as bright as a dollar. Had the whole family history at his fingers' ends. It 's a puzzling case."

"Did he tell you how he came in such a condition?" asked Mrs. Middleton.

"No, he said the story was a long and horrible one, so I sent William for some clothes for him, and the boy himself to the bathroom. We shall see how he looks when he gets cleaned up. It may be wrong, Clara, but I wish to Heaven I had never seen him."

"I don't blame you, Alfred," was her answer.

How good that bathroom looked to Lawrence! He filled the tub with water as hot as he could bear, jerked off his filthy clothes, and was quickly in the tub scrubbing himself. He wondered how any one could be as dirty as he was. The water soon became black. He let it run out, and filled the tub again. This he did four times before he became fully satisfied he was clean.

By the time he was through, William was knocking at the door, and Lawrence opened it wide enough for him to pass through a good fat parcel. It did not take him long to get inside of a fine suit of clothes which fitted him to perfection. Everything was complete, even to a necktie. When he was fully dressed, Lawrence surveyed himself in the glass, and seemed to be fully satisfied with the image he saw.

He found William waiting at the door, and that

worthy stared at him, rubbed his eyes, and stared again. Was that the same boy he had taken to the bathroom? That boy was a dirty street Arab. The boy who stood before him was as neat-looking a little gentleman as he had ever seen. It is wonderful what a transformation soap, water, and clothes will work.

William was much more condescending. "What be yo' name, young massa?" he asked.

"Lawrence."

"Well, Massa Lawrence, massa an' missy be waitin' fo' you," and he conducted Lawrence into the library, where Mr. and Mrs. Middleton were sitting. If William had been surprised at the change in the looks of Lawrence, they were more so. They could hardly believe their eyes. A boy stood before them of whom any one might be proud, a manly, sturdy fellow. He saluted his uncle and aunt gracefully, and remained standing.

"Sit down, Lawrence," said his uncle kindly. Then he spoke in a low tone to his wife. She nodded assent to what he said.

"Before we hear your story, Lawrence," said his uncle, "we will have dinner, as the servant has just announced it is ready, and you may be hungry."

"I have eaten nothing since breakfast," Lawrence replied, "and that was — " he stopped.

"Was what?" asked his uncle, somewhat curious.

"The fare dealt out to the colored deck-hands,

which they kindly shared with me to keep me from starving," he replied.

Eating food dealt out to the slaves! Mr. and Mrs. Middleton looked at one another in consternation. What had the boy been through?

"The quicker we get where there is something to eat the better," said his uncle rising.

All the way to the dining-room, Mrs. Middleton was wondering what kind of table-manners this strange boy had. Lawrence acquitted himself as a well-mannered boy should. Even the supercilious William could find no fault, except in the quantity he ate.

After dinner Lawrence told his story, and he told it simply and effectively. When he came to the story of the mob, Mr. Middleton was visibly affected.

"Great God!" he exclaimed, "a brother of mine subjected to such an indignity."

Lawrence would have passed over the painful subject with as few words as possible, but by many questions his uncle brought out all the facts of his heroism. When he came to tell how Judge Lindsly had shown pity, and had taken them in, Lawrence was eloquent.

"Judge Lindsly of Platte County?" asked his uncle.

"Yes, sir."

"Why, I know him! He is a good man."

"Good!" exclaimed Lawrence, "he is more than good, he is great. When he faced that mob that came to lynch father, I could think of nothing but one of those old Grecian or Roman gods of mythology."

"Then you have read mythology," said his uncle.

"Yes, father was very fond of it, and we used to read it together."

When he came to tell of his father's death, Lawrence's voice broke, and it was some time before he could go on. "You know father lived a short time after he was shot. It was then he told me to come to you. He — said you had quarrelled, but that he was more to blame than you, and he wanted you and Mrs. Middleton to forgive him."

Mr. Middleton arose and paced the room with quick nervous steps. The story of his brother's death, and how in his dying moments he had asked forgiveness, greatly affected him.

At last he turned, and asked in sudden fury, "What became of the wretch who shot him? Did John Brown kill him?"

"No," replied Lawrence in a low voice, "I shot him."

"You?" echoed Mr. and Mrs. Middleton in unison.

"Yes. Don't think too hard of me, uncle."

"Think hard of you!" exclaimed Mr. Middleton.

"Why, Lawrence, you are a true Middleton! The Middletons come of stern Puritan stock." He stopped and looked at his wife. "I hope I have lost my Puritanism, Clara, but not the courage of the old Puritans," he added.

She smiled, but did not answer.

Last of all came the story of the trip down the river.

"And all the troubles and death of my poor brother were brought upon him on account of his fanaticism on the question of slavery," exclaimed Mr. Middleton.

Then turning to Lawrence, he said, "My poor boy, after what you have gone through, you must be very tired. Go to bed now, and in the morning I will see what can be done for you. Neither do I feel like talking more. The story of your father's death has greatly affected me."

Lawrence gladly accepted the opportunity to retire, for the excitement of the day had completely exhausted him.

"He makes me think of Harry," said Mrs. Middleton, with a sigh. Harry was a son they had lost some years before. "My heart has already gone out to him. Of course you will give him a home, Alfred?"

"That depends on how much of his father's fanatical opinions of slavery he has imbibed," replied Mr. Middleton. "I shall see he does not suffer, but to make him one of the family I will not, if he is a carping Abolitionist. I like the boy; he is one to be proud of — a hero, I might say. The rescue of his father was wonderful, and to think of his shooting his father's slayer. Clara, I want to keep him if I can."

"I hope we can," was her answer.

A good night's rest did wonders for Lawrence, and he felt like a new boy. After breakfast, he was called into the library, by his uncle.

"Lawrence, I have called you in here to have a thorough understanding with you. You are young, but I believe wise beyond your years. I shall see that you are cared for, but whether you remain as a member of my family or not, depends on certain conditions. At present, you can hardly realize how different the conditions are here, and in the North.

"Your father not only thought slavery a moral wrong, but was, I am sorry to say, a fanatic upon the subject. That fanaticism not only brought upon him all his troubles, but caused his untimely death. That I had a brother mixed up in the Kansas troubles, and a follower of John Brown, I do not care to have known.

"If you come to me, you must never let it be known how your father died. You can simply say he is dead, and that you came to me as your only living relative. You can say he was a minister and lived in Ohio. This you can say truthfully, for he never had a residence in Kansas. But his journey through Missouri, and how he died must be a sealed book. Do you understand?"

"I think I do," replied Lawrence in a trembling voice. "I can never forget my father, but if I could blot out the remembrance of those horrible days, I would gladly do so."

"That is right," said Mr. Middleton, much gratified at his answer. "Your father was a noble but mistaken man. From what you say, I think he saw his mistake in his dying hour. No, Lawrence, do not forget him, but here, never speak of his connection with the Kansas troubles.

"One thing more. I do not know how much of his hatred of slavery you have imbibed. I do not seek to control your private belief. Now you are here, you can study the institution for yourself; but I will have no disruptions in my own house. If you do not believe in it, keep still and say nothing. I trust you see the wisdom of what I ask. It would create much unfavorable criticism, if a member of my own household were continually talking on the evils of slavery."

Lawrence thought of the advice Mr. Harmon had given him, and said, "As long as I am an inmate of your house, I will do as you wish. Whatever I may believe on the subject of slavery, it would do no good to discuss it here."

"You are a sensible boy, Lawrence. I am greatly

pleased with you," said his uncle. "Now as to my plans. You will be as one of the family. I will educate you, see that you are established in some profession or business. After that you should care for yourself."

"It is more than I could ask," replied Lawrence, deeply moved.

"Did your father have any property, except the few hundred dollars he took with him to Kansas?" asked his uncle.

"He had a house, and some money in the bank, two thousand dollars he told me. But as it was in the bank my worthless bills were on, I think that is all gone."

"Probably," replied his uncle, "but I will see what can be saved. I think it is all settled now."

"Yes, sir," said Lawrence, "and I cannot tell you how grateful I am."

"It is all right," answered his uncle, "and henceforth I am your Uncle Alfred."

"And I am your Aunt Clara," said Mrs. Middleton, who had just come into the room.

Lawrence ran to her, and buried his face in her lap, where he wept tears of joy. It was so good once more to feel the soft caress of a woman, and to be loved!

Lawrence now learned he had two cousins, Annette, a young lady of eighteen who was just finishing her education at a boarding school, and Edward, a boy of fifteen, who was in a private school preparing for college, which he would be able to enter the coming year.

"One thing I forgot," said his uncle, "and that is you are never to speak to your cousins of the Kansas matter. I will satisfy their curiosity, as much as they need know. Edward is a proud, high-spirited boy, and young as he is, is already quite a politician, and devoted to the interests of the South. I am glad he is not at home, for if he knew all, it might make some difference in how he would receive you."

And here in this luxurious home, surrounded by those who learned to love him dearly, we will leave Lawrence for four years, after which there opened up to him a new life, one full of adventures and dangers.

CHAPTER IX

FOUR YEARS AFTER

THE Fall of 1860 found Lawrence a stalwart boy of sixteen. The four years in which he had been a member of his uncle's household had been happy ones. His cousin Annette was married, and had a home of her own, her husband being a prominent lawyer and politician of New Orleans. His cousin Edward, between whom and Lawrence a very warm friendship existed, was finishing his senior year at an Eastern college. Lawrence was one of the most popular students in the academy he attended. Not only was he the foremost student, but he excelled in all athletic sports.

During those four years his uncle never alluded to the question of slavery or discussed it with him; and Lawrence, true to his promise, never spoke of those dark days he had experienced in Missouri and Kansas. But the memory of his father was ever present in his mind.

The kindness with which the slaves were used in his uncle's house did not close his eyes to the evils of the institution. He saw human beings put on the auction block, and sold; husbands parted from their wives, and children from their parents. His uncle had taken him South two or three times during the four years, and there he saw slaves driven to their daily task like dumb brutes, and once he saw a slave cruelly flogged by a brutal overseer. He also saw that the South was firmly wedded to the institution, that they believed it right, and of divine origin. Not for a moment did he believe that the gentle aunt, whom he loved as a mother, thought it wrong to own slaves, and nothing would have tempted him to say a word to hurt her feelings.

In the four years which had passed, there occurred but few incidents in the life of Lawrence which we need mention. When he had been at his uncle's a few months, he one evening attended a child's party. Among the guests he was astonished to see the little miss who had befriended him on the steamboat. He ascertained that her name was Lola' Laselle, and securing an introduction, danced with her. Not for a moment did she suspect that her well dressed, gentlemanly little partner was the ragged, dirty boy of the steamboat. Afterwards Lawrence saw her quite frequently, and they became great friends.

After he had been with his uncle about two years, a messenger came to the academy which he attended, saying he was wanted at home, and that the family carriage was waiting for him.

"What is it, John?" he asked the coachman, as he hurriedly obeyed the summons. "Is any one sick?"

"No one sick, Massa Lawrence," answered the

coachman. "Massa Middleton, he brought strange gemman home wid him. Perhaps he wanted to see young Massa."

Wondering who might want to see him, Lawrence was driven hastily home, and going into the parlor, who should be sitting there talking with his uncle, but Judge Lindsly?

He waited for no introduction, but rushing forward, seized the Judge's hand, and raised it to his lips, and his tears fell upon it. He tried to speak, but could only stammer his joy of the meeting.

Judge Lindsly was greatly moved at his reception. He wiped his eyes, and after he had scanned Lawrence from head to feet said: "How you have grown! You are getting to be quite a man, and your uncle gives a glowing account of you. Says you are getting to be a real Missourian.

"Little did I think," said the Judge turning to Mr. Middleton, " when I opened my doors, and took this boy and his father in, that I was befriending your brother and nephew. What are you thinking of making of the boy, Middleton? A banker?"

"No!" answered his uncle, " he wants to be a lawyer, and I am educating him with that in view."

"Good! good!" exclaimed the Judge, "a noble profession, and he will be an honor to it."

"If I can only become as great and good a lawyer as you," said Lawrence, "the height of my ambition will be reached."

"Oh, you flatterer!" laughed the Judge, "you must aspire higher than that." But he seemed to be well pleased.

Lawrence had a multitude of questions to ask, and one of the first was, "How is good Doctor Good-now?"

"As fat and jolly as ever. He often speaks of you, and rejoices over your good fortune."

"Why, has he heard of me since I left?" asked Lawrence in surprise.

"There, I reckon I have left the cat out of the bag," said the Judge, looking at Mr. Middleton.

"I don't mind telling you now, Lawrence," said his uncle, "that I wrote to Judge Lindsly when you first came. I wanted to substantiate the remarkable story you told, and also to thank Judge Lindsly for his heroic defence of my brother."

"Then the Judge and the Doctor have known all this time where I was," said Lawrence.

"Yes, but I thought it best for them not to write. I wanted you to forget that horrible experience," answered his uncle.

"Now that I know it," said Lawrence, "Judge, will you not give my heartfelt gratitude to the Doctor, and tell him, that of all the persons in the world, except you, I had rather shake his hand."

"That I will," answered the Judge.

The conversation now became more general. In speaking of the border warfare, the Judge said it was not so fierce as it had been under the administration of President Pierce, and gave it as his opinion that Kansas would eventually come in as a free State. Both he and Mr. Middleton took a gloomy view of the future of the country, and both agreed that the South was being sorely tried.

"I love the old flag," said the Judge, "and it would be a sad day, if it should cease to float over me; but, Middleton, secession is in the air; I feel it. And if it should come, what can such as you and I do? What ought we to do?"

"If that day ever comes, which I hope it never will," answered Mr. Middleton slowly, "although I am of Northern birth, I should have to stay with the South."

"And I should have to do the same," said the Judge, "but let us hope that the North will see the justice of the demands of the South, and grant them."

This conversation Lawrence remembered for a long time. Was war impending between the North and the South? He had never thought of it in that light before. Before the Judge left, Lawrence asked for a private interview with him, which was readily granted.

"It 's about father," said Lawrence, with some hesitation.

"Please, don't speak about it if it pains you," said the Judge kindly.

" But I must," answered Lawrence, " for it is to do justice to his memory that I speak. During the few days that he lived after we left, I often heard him allude to it. He was in fear that you might think that in some way he was instrumental in getting George to run away. It was a bitter thought to him, after all you had done for us."

"I never entertained such an idea. I am sorry your father thought so," answered the Judge.

" Father never knew George was with the party," continued Lawrence, " until we reached the river, and then he tried so hard to get him to go back with the horses; but John Brown would not listen to it, said it would be a mortal sin to send a man back into slavery. But I think poor George has regretted many a time that he ever left you."

" Why, what makes you think so? " asked the Judge.

" Have you never heard from him since he left?"

"No, why do you ask?"

Then Lawrence told him of seeing George on the steamboat, and what he had said.

" So those scoundrels captured him, sold him, and kept the money," exclaimed the Judge, with some heat. " I will make Travers smart for it yet, if I can get any proof."

When the Judge departed it was with a promise from Lawrence that some day he would try and visit him.

"Spend a vacation with me," said the Judge, "you will enjoy it."

About this time there came another incident into the life of Lawrence which ever after influenced him. The great debate between Lincoln and Douglas was being held, and they were to speak at Alton.

Mr. Middleton was a great admirer of Douglas, and signified his intention of attending the debate. Lawrence asked permission to accompany him, which was readily granted.

Douglas's well rounded periods, and sonorous sentences made little impression on him, but every word that Lincoln spoke, burned into his very soul. Here was a man that believed as his father had done, and who had the courage of his convictions, and forced them home with convincing logic. That speech went a long way toward making Lawrence what he became.

In 1859 came John Brown's ill-fated and insane raid on Harper's Ferry. Lawrence had heard little of him since leaving Kansas, but now the papers were filled with the account of the raid. The South could not, or would not, but believe that his raid was backed by a powerful Northern organization, and for a time the excitement ran high. His trial and execution speedily followed, and when the end came, Lawrence dropped a tear to his memory. His raid could be looked upon only as the act of an insane man, and there came to his mind the words of Doctor Goodnow, "Brown, your fanaticism will get you hanged some day."

The Fall of 1860 found the country in the throes of another presidential election. The Republican party stronger, more united than ever in its opposition to the extension of slavery, had for its standard-bearer, Abraham Lincoln.

The Democratic party was rent and torn with factional strife. The slavery question had grown to gigantic proportions. The South was demanding more and more; the North was disposed to grant less.

Stephen A. Douglas, the Little Giant of Illinois, in his ambition to become President, endeavored to conciliate the South. To accomplish this, he it was who forced the repeal of the Missouri Compromise, and made it possible for Kansas to become a slave State.

But in his debate with Lincoln, he had been forced by that astute politician to answer a certain question, and Douglas answered it in a way which did not please the South. Moreover, his Kansas-Nebraska bill had filled the nation with strife and in no way had helped the South; therefore the South would have none of him, and bolted the Democratic convention, nominating as their candidate John C. Breckenridge on a strong pro-slavery platform.

The regular convention nominated Douglas on a compromise platform.

Conservative men of all parties saw that a crisis was coming, and an Independent convention was called, and a platform adopted denouncing the extreme measures of both the Republican and the Democratic parties, and John Bell of Tennessee was nominated. Thus in the presidential campaign of 1860 there were four candidates.

The country was wild with excitement. Monster mass-meetings were held, attended by vast multitudes. Thousands of men marched in procession carrying flaming torches. The flood-gates of oratory were opened, and the country was deluged with speeches.

Although his party was divided, Douglas had hopes of being elected; he made a strong appeal to the country, claiming that his election was the only salvation for the Union.

Lincoln did not dodge the situation, offered no compromise. "A house divided against itself," he cried, "cannot stand. This nation must eventually become all slave, or all free. Which shall it be?" He declared that the Republican party had no intention of disturbing slavery where it was, but there must be no more slave territory.

The South claimed that all the Territories should be open to slavery, and thus the issues were joined. "Elect Lincoln, and we will withdraw from the Union, as we have a perfect right to do under the Constitution," was the threat which the South con-

He received a blow between the eyes that sent him sprawling

Lola, handing Lawrence a paper, "Sign that and we will elect you captain. We boys have been talking it over."

Lawrence shook his head. "No, Leon," he said, "I prefer not to join any club. We are having altogether too much politics for the good of our studies. Let our elders attend to the politics."

Leon looked disappointed as the paper was returned to him. "I am sorry," he said, "you will be an odd fish, Lawrence, if you join none of the clubs."

"I know why he don't join," said a boy by the name of Benton Shelley, and the leader of the Breckenridge forces. "I asked him to join our club, and he almost insulted me."

"What's the reason?" shouted a dozen voices.

"Boys," said Shelley, drawing himself up with importance, "all the time that Lawrence Middleton has attended this academy, did any of you ever hear him say one word on politics? Did you ever know him to take any part in our discussion on the rights of the South? Hasn't he been as dumb as an oyster on the subject of slavery?"

"That's so! that's so!" shouted the boys, "but we never thought of it before. What's the reason, Lawrence?"

"I will tell you the reason," said young Shelley with a sneer. "At heart he is a Lincolnite, but he hasn't the grit to say so. He is not only a Lincolnite, but a coward."

Hardly were the words out of his mouth before he received a blow between the eyes which sent him sprawling. He staggered to his feet, and with a howl of rage made for Lawrence, but this time received a blow which completely knocked him out.

The campus was in an uproar. "A fight! a fight!" shouted the boys, as they crowded around. But the fight was over. Young Shelley had had enough. He was helped to his feet by some of his companions, and led away, but as he went, he cast such a look of malignant hate at Lawrence that the latter knew he had made an enemy forever.

"I don't blame Middleton a bit," cried one of the boys. "I believe I would shoot any one who called me a Lincolnite."

"And I! And I," shouted a dozen others.

Lawrence saw that his blow was misunderstood; it was the word "coward" which had stung him. But he saw that the time was coming when he would be obliged to take a stand.

CHAPTER X

LAWRENCE TAKES A STAND

THE great political battle was at an end, and by their ballots the American people had elected Abraham Lincoln President of the United States.

Of all the States in the Union, Missouri alone gave her electoral vote to Douglas. Lincoln received only seventeen thousand votes in the State to Breckenridge's thirty-one thousand. Bell received, within a few hundred, as many votes as Douglas, which showed the State to be overwhelmingly conservative.

The other border slave States gave their electoral votes to Bell. They did not sympathize with the fire-eaters of the South.

There was great rejoicing in the North over the election of Lincoln. Bonfires blazed, and cannon thundered. Wide-Awakes marched, with their flaming torches, by tens of thousands, and made the welkin ring with their shouts of victory. But amid all the rejoicing there was a great dread over the land. Would the South make good her threats, and secede from the Union? The great majority of the people of the North thought not. They could not imagine the South would attempt anything so suicidal; but there were thousands who looked into each other's face with anxious hearts, and asked, "What next?"

The country had not long to wait. The election of Lincoln caused a frenzy of rage to sweep over the entire South. The fire-eaters received the news of his election with as much joy as did the Republicans of the North. It was just what they wanted and had worked for, longed for. Now they could carry out their long-cherished plan of withdrawing from the Union. But to the great mass of the Southern people, the election of Lincoln was as a deadly blow given by a friend. They loved the Union, but the whole North had turned against them. The Government their forefathers had helped to create, and had shed their blood for, they believed had become a tyrant to oppress them; therefore they turned from the flag which sheltered them, and gave ear to the fiery speeches, and fierce denunciations of the fire-eaters.

South Carolina set the ball rolling, and passed an Ordinance of Secession, December 20. The people went wild when the act was passed, and a wave of enthusiasm swept over the State. Little did they imagine the untold woe they were bringing on the Nation by reason of their rash act. The other cotton States were not slow in following the example of South Carolina, and before the year 1861 was a month old, had passed ordinances of secession.

The border slave States still clung to the Union, hoping against hope that the conflict might be averted and the Union preserved; but the extreme South would not listen, neither would the North give up every principle for which they had fought and won.

On the fourth of February, delegates from the States which had seceded met in convention at Montgomery, Alabama, elected Jefferson Davis President of the newly formed Confederate States, and what they believed to be a new nation was formally launched.

If there had been a Jackson in the Presidential chair, the rebellion might have been crushed in the beginning. But Buchanan, weak and vacillating, saw the nation crumbling, and sat and wrung his hands in impotency, as the ruins fell around him. "The South has no right to secede," he wailed, "but as she has seceded, I have no right to coerce her back into the Union."

Notwithstanding that the cotton States had set up a government of their own, there were still a multitude of people who believed that the war might be averted, and the seceding States brought back. Peace meetings were held all over the country. There had yet no Patrick Henry arisen to thunder, "Gentlemen may cry 'Peace, peace,' but there is no peace; the war has actually begun." It had begun nearly ten years before, along the borders of Kansas and Missouri, but the nation had closed its eyes to the fact. Now the day of reckoning had come. Freedom and slavery were to grapple in a death struggle. Lincoln was right, the country had to be all free, or all slave.

In the border States, a terrific struggle was going on. The people of those States knew if war came, it would be they who would suffer the most, and they appealed to both North and South to stay their hands. Nowhere was the approach of war looked upon with more apprehension than in Missouri. Surrounded on three sides by free States, the inhabitants knew that if war came, their country would be overrun with hostile troops; that neighbor would be against neighbor, brother against brother, son against father. No wonder they feared and trembled as the war clouds gathered.

Claiborne F. Jackson had been elected Governor of Missouri on the Douglas ticket. Jackson possessed many characteristics of Old Hickory. Nothing daunted him in carrying out his designs. Although elected on the Douglas ticket, he proved as ardent a secessionist as Jefferson Davis himself. In his inaugural address, given when but South Carolina had seceded, he said: "Missouri will, in my opinion, best consult her own interests, and the interests of the whole country, by a timely declaration of her determination to stand by her sister slaveholding States."

And from that time Governor Jackson did everything in his power to drag Missouri out of the Union. The Legislature was with him, and they had no more thought but that, if given the opportunity, the State would declare for secession, than they had that the sun would cease to shine; so they called for delegates to be elected to a State convention to consider the question. This was to keep up the semblance of the doctrine of State Rights. The Union men of the State lost no time in meeting the issue. At the head of the Unconditional Union men of St. Louis, was Frank P. Blair, Jr., and to him the Nation owes its everlasting gratitude for what he did and what he accomplished.

The election took place February 18, and the State declared for the Union by 80,000 majority. Not one outspoken secessionist was elected to the convention. So crushing was the defeat that for a time Jackson and his followers were confounded; but they soon rallied, and as all the State machinery was in their hands, they tried to accomplish by intrigue, deceit, and force what they could not by the will of the people.

Throwing the doctrine of State Rights to the winds, Governor Jackson boldly declared his intention of taking the State out of the Union, it making no difference to him how great a majority were against it. Now began a battle for the control of the State that for intensity was not equalled in any other in the Union. Governor Jackson waged a battle worthy of a better cause, and he would have been successful, if it had not been for two men: Frank P. Blair and General Nathaniel Lyon. In these two men, Governor Jackson found opponents as brave, as bold, as daring as he.

Lawrence Middleton could not remain silent in the midst of such excitement. His uncle up to the time of the convention had acted with the conservative Union men. He still hoped that by wise statesmanship the storm might be averted. Lawrence spoke to his uncle, and asked him if it would be a violation of his promise if he declared himself for the Union, saying it was impossible for him to remain silent any longer on the question in which all were absorbed.

"No, Lawrence," said his uncle, "I am in favor of the Union as long as there is any Union to be preserved. But I believe the South is justified in demanding her rights. I still hope for peace, I cannot believe that the people of the North have entirely lost their senses, and that they will make war on the South."

"But, uncle, if there should be war?" asked Lawrence.

"If the Federal Government attempts to coerce the South, if it sends a hostile force in our midst, there will be but one course for me to pursue," answered his uncle, "I shall be with the South."

Lawrence said no more, but from that day, he was known as a stanch Union advocate.

"So Benton Shelley was right after all," sneered one of his schoolmates. "You are a Lincolnite, and have been all the time."

"To be for the Union is not to be a Lincolnite," answered Lawrence hotly. "There are thousands of men here in St. Louis who voted for Douglas or Bell, and now are heart and soul for the Union. But if it suits you any better, I will say that Abraham Lincoln has been lawfully elected President of the United States, and that every true loyal person will support him as such. I for one will."

"Support the dirty buffoon if you want to," angrily answered his opponent, "but he will never be President of the South, mark that."

"Come, come, boys," spoke up Arthur Reel, a friend of Lawrence but of Southern proclivities, "don't quarrel. If war come, we will all get our fill."

"Do you think the Yankees will fight?" asked an anxious-faced boy. "Brother belongs to the Minute Men, and he is afraid there will be no fighting; says the Yankees will run like sheep."

"Don't let your brother worry," said Reel, with a laugh, "they will not run half fast enough to suit him. But there is the bell, boys, and if the Yankees are as tough as my Greek and Latin, I for one don't want to meet them."

At this the boys all laughed, and trooped into the schoolroom. But from that day Lawrence noticed that he was avoided by the Southern element of the school. Boys he knew well would pass without speaking. He met sinister glances, and contemptuous looks. All this was galling to his proud spirit, but as no real insult was offered, he could do nothing.

Lawrence was not the only one who suffered from ostracism. One day he met Lola Laselle on the street; she was wiping tears from her eyes, and Lawrence saw she had been crying bitterly.

"Why, Miss Lola, what is the matter?" he asked, much concerned. "Has any one hurt you?"

"It 's that mean Dorothy Hamilton," she sobbed; "you know she and I have always been the best of friends."

"Yes, I know," said Lawrence. "Bosom friends, I believe; had no secrets from one another."

"Well, what do you think?" continued Lola. "I met her just now, and she told me never to speak to her again; that my father and brother were Lincolnites, and that I should go and associate with the Dutch, where I belonged. And she lied. Father is no Lincolnite; he voted for Douglas."

"I hope your father and brother are for the Union," said Lawrence.

"Yes, they are, and that is the reason Dorothy called them Lincolnites. Are you for the Union?"

"Now, and forever," answered Lawrence.

"Oh! goody! goody!" cried the girl. "Now I wonder what Dorothy will have to say!"

"What has Dorothy got to do with my being for the Union?" asked Lawrence, a little puzzled.

"Why, she told me — but, my! that's a secret. I promised never to tell."

"I thought you and Dorothy had quarrelled; that she had cut you cold. Promises ought not to hold in such cases." Lawrence's logic was faulty, but he wanted to get at the secret.

"I don't care if I do tell, the mean thing," exclaimed Lola, throwing all scruples to the winds. "She said you were the nicest boy she knew, and that she had set her cap for you, and that she was going to marry you some day."

"Now, I call that right nice in Dorothy," said Lawrence. "Let's see, she is as much as thirteen; but I can afford to wait, for Dorothy is really a very pretty girl."

"I know of lots prettier," replied Lola with a curl of the lip.

"And Miss Lola Laselle is one of them, I suppose," said Lawrence, teasingly.

"Now, Lawrence Middleton, you are making fun of me, and I don't like you," and Lawrence saw the little chin quiver, and the tears gather in her eyes.

He saw that he had hurt her feelings, and

instantly repented. "There, Lola, I was only fooling," he made haste to reply. "The first time I ever saw you, I not only thought you were one of the prettiest, but one of the kindest-hearted little girls I ever saw."

Lola looked puzzled. "The first time I ever remember seeing you, was at a party," she answered. "I danced with you, and thought you a very nice little boy."

"Thank you, for the compliment, but it was not at the party; it was before that."

Lola looked more puzzled than ever. "I never remember seeing you before the party," she said. "Where was it?"

"It's a secret."

"I love secrets."

"But you will tell, you have just told me one of Dorothy's secrets."

"You made me, you mean thing, but I will never tell yours, Lawrence, cross my heart I won't."

"Do you remember that four years ago last fall, you came down the Missouri River in a steamboat?"

"Yes, I remember that. Mother and I had been to St. Joseph visiting. It was an awful poky trip. We got off of the boat at Jefferson City, and came the rest of the way on the cars."

"There was a little boy on that boat," continued Lawrence, "who had only deck passage, and not knowing any better, he wandered into the cabin, and received a cuff from the mate which sent him rolling."

"Yes, I remember that, but—"

"Hold on, and let me tell the rest, first," broke in Lawrence. "A certain little girl saw the blow, and she stamped her foot, and shook her tiny fist at the mate, and cried: 'You bad, bad man to strike a 'ittle boy!'"

"Lawrence Middleton, how did you know this?" cried Lola in astonishment. "My! how mamma did shake me!"

"That is not all," continued Lawrence. "The little girl came up to the boy, and said: 'I am sorry, 'ittle boy; did the bad man hurt you?'"

"Lawrence Middleton, tell me this minute how you know this," exclaimed Lola, all excitement.

"I was that little boy."

"Lawrence Middleton, you are joking!"

"Not at all. How did I know this, if I was not there? I knew you the moment I saw you at that party four years ago, and that is the reason I sought an introduction. I meant to tell you sometime, but not as soon as this."

"How did you come to take deck passage?" she asked, wonderingly.

"The story is a short one," replied Lawrence. "My father died in Kansas, and before he died, he made me promise to come to my uncle Alfred. Just before I was to take passage my money was stolen, or the same as stolen, and I only had enough left to pay deck passage."

Lola clapped her hands and fairly danced. "How nice!" she cried. "It's just like a story book."

"I did n't think it very nice at the time," replied Lawrence. "The only bright thing in the whole trip to me was your sympathy, little girl."

"Little girl! little girl!" mimicked Lola, drawing herself up to her full height. "I will let you know, sir, I am going on thirteen, most as old as Dorothy Hamilton."

"Pardon me! I meant the little girl who took my part. Do you blame me for thinking her one of the sweetest and best little girls I ever saw? And Lola, I have not changed my mind much in four years," and laughing, he bade her good-day, and left her before she had time to reply.

The little girl's face was rosy, and she tripped away as lightly as if she had never quarrelled with Dorothy Hamilton.

As fate would have it, Lawrence had not gone two blocks before he met this same Dorothy Hamilton. Although but a few months older, she was a much larger girl than Lola Laselle. She had dark, lustrous eyes and a wealth of brown hair in which there were glints of gold. Her features were quite regular, and she gave promise of great beauty when she should grow into womanhood.

No sooner did she see Lawrence than she cried:
"Lawrence Middleton, I am so glad to see you, for
I have just heard something about you that I can't
believe — I won't believe; tell me it is not true."

"What in the world is it?" asked Lawrence pre-
tending great surprise; "that I have robbed a bank,
or murdered my grandmother?"

"Oh! worse than that."

"Worse than that? Stealing chickens, then."

"Much worse. I heard — I heard you were a
Black Republican; that you were against the South,
and for Lincoln."

"Perfectly awful!" said Lawrence drawing down
his face. "Now, if I had only stolen chickens —"

"I knew it was a lie, I knew it was a lie," broke
in the girl, with a radiant face. "How I hate the old
flag. Do you know what I did this morning?"

"How should I know? Not anything as awful as
I am accused of, I hope."

"I spit on the Yankee flag, and then trampled it
in the mud. I tell you I stamped hard."

"I am sorry for that," replied Lawrence gravely.

"Sorry? — why?" asked the girl in surprise.

"Because the flag you tried to dishonor is not a
Yankee flag. It is the flag of our country, of both
North and South. It is the flag under which you
and I were born, and we should reverence it."

"Then it is all true what I heard," she cried.
"Lawrence Middleton, I despise you; you are a

traitor to the South. Go and consort with the low-down Dutch they say you have taken up with."

"Germans," corrected Lawrence.

"Germans or Dutch — what's the difference? They are a low-down set," she cried, with flashing eyes. "I am disappointed in you, Lawrence Middleton. I thought you were a man. I never want to see you again. Never speak to me."

"You seem to be cutting all your old acquaintances to-day, Miss Dorothy."

"Why, how do you know?"

"I met a little girl up the street a few moments ago, and she was crying bitterly because her bosom friend had cut her cold."

"I suppose you mean Lola Laselle. Of course you comforted her," she replied, scornfully.

"Sure, I told her it was only jealousy that made you act as you did, because she is prettier than you," Lawrence answered maliciously.

"Perhaps her style of beauty pleases you with your low tastes," snapped Dorothy. "Never speak to me again!" And with this parting shot she left him.

But as she turned to go, Lawrence saw that her eyes were filled with tears. They were tears of anger, mortification, and — well, that was a secret with Dorothy.

CHAPTER XI

THE SWORD OF BUNKER HILL

TO the Germans of St. Louis belongs the honor of saving Missouri to the Union. It needed a Frank P. Blair and a General Lyon to lead them, but without their help these two men would have been powerless. True to their adopted country, the Germans never wavered in their allegiance to the Union. The flag they had sworn to uphold was their flag, and they knew no other. Well might the native American hang his head in shame, when he turned against the flag under which he was born, and saw it upheld with such devotion by citizens of foreign birth.

During the political campaign of the fall before, Frank P. Blair had been instrumental in forming the Germans into Wide-Awake companies. After the election, he kept these organizations intact, and turned them into semi-military companies. Thus he had the nucleus of an army at hand. Blair was never deceived by the illusive cry of peace. He knew the Southern people, how deadly in earnest they were, and felt that war would come. Therefore he was among the first to prepare for it. He was to Missouri what General Nelson was to Kentucky.

The hatred of the secessionists toward the Germans was intense. They denounced them as beer-drinkers, and above all as atheists, haters of God and religion, especially of the Catholic Church. Thus in St. Louis the religious question, as well as the slavery question entered into the controversy. The secessionists made the most of this condition, and succeeded in turning the majority of the Irish in the city to the Confederate side. But not all, for many a gallant Irishman saw through the ruse, and remained true to the Union.

Attending the same school as Lawrence, was a German boy named Carl Mayer. He was a bright scholar, and spoke English as fluently as a native. He and Lawrence were great friends. He had taught Lawrence the German language, so that at the outbreak of the war Lawrence was a fine German scholar. This proved of great service to him in the work he was called upon to do.

Early in January, Carl left school, as his proud spirit could not brook the foul insults he continually heard hurled against the German people by the boys of Southern proclivities.

Shortly after Lawrence had come out boldly for the Union, he met Carl one day, the latter seeming overjoyed to see him.

"I hear you are for the Union," he said.

"Every time," answered Lawrence, shaking Carl by the hand heartily.

"How would you like to join a company of Home Guards?" asked Carl. "You know the Southern boys are forming companies they call Minute Men. Frank Blair is forming four regiments of Home Guards, mostly Germans, but with a fair sprinkling of Americans. In some of the companies are a great many boys from sixteen to twenty years of age. I belong to a company. There are quite a number of Americans in the company, and we want one of the lieutenants to be an American. If you will join, I believe you can get the position."

"Am I not too young for an officer?" asked Lawrence.

"Rather young, but you would readily pass for eighteen. The company meets to-night to organize. Blair will be there. What do you say? Come and join us."

After a little consideration, Lawrence agreed to attend the meeting that night, but whether he would join or not, — he must think that over.

When Lawrence repaired to the hall to his surprise he was stopped at the door by a sentinel who asked him to give his name and residence. He did so, and the sentinel shook his head, saying he could not enter unless some one would vouch for him.

"Vouch for what?" asked Lawrence.

"That you are for the Union and the flag," was the answer. "Is there any one here you know?"

"I came here by the invitation of Carl Mayer,"

answered Lawrence, somewhat nettled, "but if you don't want me I can go away."

"Carl Mayer, das ist goot," said the sentinel.

Carl was called, and readily vouched for the newcomer. Lawrence was told their portals had to be very carefully guarded, to prevent the entrance of spies. "No one is admitted," said Carl, "unless he is known to be a true Union man."

Lawrence found about a hundred present, most of them stalwart young men, and a few boys not older than he. No sooner was it known who Lawrence was, than he was received with rousing cheers. To get a Middleton in their ranks, one who moved in the most aristocratic circle of the city, was something not to be overlooked. Lawrence saw that they already considered him as one of them, yet he had come almost decided not to join, for fear his uncle would not like it. But Frank Blair made a speech, and before he was half through, Lawrence's youthful heart was fired, and he resolved that come what would, the day for silence had passed, that he would not only be for the Union, but would fight for it, if necessary; and he was among the first to sign the roll.

But the new company must have officers, and when it came to the selection of a second lieutenant, Carl Mayer arose and nominated Lawrence Middleton, making a speech in his favor which was received with cheers.

Lawrence pleaded his youth and inexperience, and declared he was perfectly content to serve in the ranks.

"You are young," said Blair, "but you have all the appearance of being at least eighteen. I am also told that you speak German fluently, which will be a great help to you in this company; not only that, but your example may influence some of your associates to declare for the Union."

This decided the question, and Lawrence was duly elected Second Lieutenant, to the great joy of Carl Mayer, who was made a sergeant. After the election of officers, the company was put through a short drill by an army officer present, and then dismissed with the understanding that they were to meet three times a week for drill.

Lawrence and Carl left the hall together. They had much to talk about, and without a single thought of danger they were walking along, when, as they were passing a dark alley, two men sprang out and attacked them. Although taken by surprise, the two boys defended themselves valiantly, and soon put their assailants to flight. But the skirmish had left marks on them. Lawrence was nursing a sore head, and Carl had a bloody nose, and a black eye.

"If I mistake not," said Lawrence, "the fellow that went for me was Benton Shelley. But if I meet him to-morrow I shall know, for I gave him a good one right in the eye; it put him out of business."

"I don't know who attacked me," said Carl, "but he was a good one. He got my nose and eye all right," and he carefully felt of the injured members. "Mercy! my nose is as big as two noses already. I shall be a sight by to-morrow. But I gave him a good one, right on the face, and it bowled him over like a tenpin. But his legs were good, for he ran like a deer when he got up."

"How do you suppose those fellows knew we were coming this way?" asked Lawrence.

"Spied on us," answered Carl. "There are spies watching every meeting we hold. That is why we have to be so careful. I bet every boy in the academy will know to-morrow that you have joined the Home Guards. Lawrence, I bet you leave that school before a week."

This set Lawrence thinking. It was near midnight when he got home. He met his cousin in the hall, who looked at him closely.

"What 's the matter?" he asked. "You look as if you had been in a skirmish."

"I was attacked by a footpad as I was coming home," answered Lawrence, "but I beat him off without much trouble."

"Which shows that young boys like you should n't be out so late. I think I shall have father look after your comings and goings. I am suspicious, my lad. Beware how far you go." Thus saying Edward passed into the library; and when he opened the door, late as it was, Lawrence saw that his uncle was up, and with him were four gentlemen. One of them he knew; it was General D. M. Frost, commander of the Missouri State Militia.

Once in his room, Lawrence began to reflect very seriously on what he had done. The warning given to him by his cousin, General Frost's visit to his uncle, all meant that his uncle had given up all hopes of the preservation of the Union, and was to cast his lot with the South. Lawrence felt that by joining Blair's Home Guards, he had burned all his bridges behind him; but he was not sorry, though what he had done might make him an outcast from his uncle's home.

Then the relations between him and his cousin Edward had become strained. They had always been the best of friends, like two brothers, but Edward was a regular fire-eater. He had refused to return to Yale, where he would have been graduated in a few months, saying that life among the Yankees was unbearable. "And to think of those cowardly mudsills whipping the South!" he would say: "Why, I challenged half a dozen of them for their insults, and they laughed at me. The only thing I am ashamed of is that I have Yankee blood in me."

He had joined the militia under General Frost, and was a close friend of Basil Duke, Green, and the others who were organizing the Minute Men. He had tried hard to get Lawrence to go with him, and became quite angry when Lawrence refused.

"I am for the Union," said Lawrence, "and so is your father, so I do not see why you should be angry at me."

"Father is for the South, which you are not," said Edward. "He is foolish enough to think the Union can be preserved; that the North will grant justice to the slave States, and that they will come back. He will learn better soon, and then he will be heart and soul with the South."

Lawrence sighed, for he felt that Edward spoke only the truth. "And," continued Edward, "you had better get over your Yankee notions, and that mighty quick, or this house will be altogether too hot to hold you."

"We will not quarrel, Edward," said Lawrence; "but like your father, I hope there will be no war, that it will be settled before it comes to that."

"It will never be settled until it is settled right, and that is when the South is a great and glorious nation by itself," declared Edward, with much warmth.

Lawrence thought of all this, as he sat in his room reflecting on the events of the day, with sorrow in his heart. If he had known what was taking place in the library, that sorrow would have been increased tenfold.

General D. M. Frost, like Mr. Middleton, was of Northern birth, but he was thoroughly in accord with Governor Jackson in his endeavors to drag Missouri out of the Union.

As one of the representative men of the city, General Frost had called on Mr. Middleton to find out his exact sentiments, and see if he would not aid in organizing the militia.

"I have been for the Union, and am still for it, if there is any hope of saving it," said Mr. Middleton, "but if all hope is gone, of course, I am with the South."

"There is not the slightest hope," said Frost; "the Southern States are out for good. They would not come back, if allowed to dictate their own terms. They are sick and tired of being tied to the radical North. The buffoon, smutty Lincoln can never be President of the South; and I, for one, am glad of it. The only question for Missouri to decide is, where will she stand? Will it be with the North, or her sister Southern States?"

"If it comes to that," said Mr. Middleton, "I say the South every time. But, General, does not this mean war?"

"Let it come," exclaimed Frost; "do you think for a moment that the Yankees, and these miserable Dutchmen can stand before our gallant Southern boys? Not for a moment! They will wipe them off the face of the earth."

"But war will be horrible," said Mr. Middleton. "Remember, General, that we are Northern-born, that we shall be warring against our kith and kin.

Households will be divided, even my own house. I have a nephew here whom I love almost as a son, yet I am almost sure, if war comes, he will be for the old flag."

"Yours will not be the only divided household, Mr. Middleton. Thank God it is only a nephew. Yes, as you say, war is terrible, and it will come if the North will not let the South go in peace, for go she will."

Much more was said, but when General Frost and his companions left, Mr. Middleton was committed to the Southern cause.

The next day was an anxious one to Lawrence. He resolved to tell his uncle all, and abide by the consequences, but his trial came sooner than he expected. Along in the afternoon, his cousin came into his room, wildly excited, and white with rage.

"Is it true," he demanded, "that you joined one of Frank Blair's Dutch companies last night?"

"Who told you I had joined one of Blair's companies of Home Guards?" coolly asked Lawrence.

"That is not the question," angrily replied Edward. "The question is, did you, or did you not join?"

"I deny your right to question me, but tell me who told you, and I will answer, not before."

"Benton Shelley did. He says he knows it to be a fact."

"Have you seen Shelley to-day?"

"Of course. How could he have told me, if I had not seen him?"

"Is he out, or did you see him at home?"

"Why this beating around the bush? But I saw him at home. He met with a slight accident last night."

"Had a black eye, did n't he?"

"How did you know that?" asked his cousin, somewhat astonished.

"Because it was Benton Shelley who waylaid me last night like a footpad. I was almost sure it was he, now I know. I will now answer your question. I did join one of Frank Blair's companies of Home Guards, and I do not see why I don't have as good a right to join the Home Guards, as you have to join the Minute Men."

"That settles it," stormed Edward, "this roof is not large enough to shelter both. Either you or I leave it. You are an ingrate, an —"

"Stop right where you are, Edward, call no names. It is not seemly that we should quarrel. This is a conflict of principles, not of individuals. I am for the old flag, you for the South. Neither of us can help being what we are. Let us part in peace. As for me, I cannot come between father and son. I leave this roof to-morrow, so be content."

This answer sobered Edward a little. "Go!" he

exclaimed. "Go, and joy go with you. I believe you always were an Abolitionist."

"We will not discuss slavery," replied Lawrence calmly. "I am content to leave it where it is; but when slavery raises its hand to destroy the government, I am against slavery."

"I hate the old flag, I despise the North and everything in it; I long to see the flag of the Confederacy unfurled over this State; and mark you, it will be. All the Frank Blairs and all the Dutch in the world can't prevent it," passionately exclaimed Edward.

"And to help to prevent it is the reason I am against you," replied Lawrence.

"And being against me, you are against father, against all of us. You are a traitor to those who have befriended you, cared for you. I hate the sight of you. I do not see how you can look any of us in the face."

Without waiting for Lawrence to reply, Edward went out, and slammed the door behind him. Lawrence was glad, for there was a hot reply on the end of his tongue.

"But Edward was right," he thought, "I am a beggar, a dependant on his father's bounty. I see it now. I never thought of it before. So kindly have they used me, I have felt as one of the family. It is a poor requital I am giving them, but, as God is my helper, I can do no differently. Yet it is hard, so hard, to grieve them so," and Lawrence was not ashamed of the tears which fell, fast and hot, from his eyes.

His uncle was away for the evening, and he could not see him until morning, but with a sad heart, he set about packing his things. Not another day would he be a dependant on his uncle's bounty. For the future he had no fears. He was young and strong, he would win his way. He slept but little, thinking of what he would do. He did not know that for the next four years his career was already marked out, that they would be spent amid the shock and din of battle.

Breakfast was a constrained meal. His uncle and aunt were not present. When Lawrence came in, Edward arose and left the table.

He did not have to ask to see his uncle, for a message came from him that he would like to see Lawrence in the library. Mr. Middleton was seated by a table toying with a paperweight. His face looked sad and care-worn. Lawrence thought he had never seen him look so old. He did not speak as Lawrence entered, but motioned him to a chair. Lawrence took the proffered seat, and for a full minute neither spoke. The only sound that Lawrence heard was the beating of his own heart, and it throbbed painfully.

At length Mr. Middleton said slowly, "So you and Edward have quarrelled."

"Not exactly quarrelled, uncle, but when he found I had joined the Home Guards he was frightfully angry, accused me of being a traitor to you, and said, he and I could never live under the same roof."

"Yes, I know, Edward has told me," replied his uncle coldly.

Lawrence could stand it no longer. He threw himself down by his uncle's side. "Uncle! Uncle!" he cried pleadingly, "forgive me! I ought to have told you, but I just had to join. Uncle, you have been so good to me. I wish I could be like Edward, but I cannot. I cannot fight for slavery and against the old flag. I must leave you, uncle. I must not come between you and Edward."

Mr. Middleton was visibly moved. "Lawrence," he exclaimed, brokenly, "to part with you is like parting with one of my own children. You have been a good boy, and I have had high hopes as to your future; but it is best that you go for a time. I shall not lose sight of you, and only hope that in time you may see differently, and come back to us. I am thankful you kept your temper in talking with Edward. I shudder at what might have been, if you had been as hot-headed as he."

"I do not think anything could induce me to raise a hand against him," said Lawrence earnestly, "he is the same as a brother to me."

"Thank God for that," exclaimed Mr. Middleton fervently. "Oh, this miserable, this unnatural strife! Lawrence, like you, I have had a battle with myself. Do you think it has not caused me pain to give up my country, the flag I once so loved? But the decision is made. As long as there were hopes of justice being granted the South, I was for the Union, but the fanatics of the North would not have it so. The South is out for good; Missouri's place is with the South. Henceforth the Confederate States of America is my country; the Stars and Stripes is to me a foreign flag."

"To me," said Lawrence, "the old flag represents everything dear, but that will make no difference in my love to you and yours. I believe you have decided according to what you think right. I shall always think so. And, uncle, let us part in peace. Whatever may come, let there be no war, no hate, between us personally."

"Peace it shall be, my boy. You know the history of that sword there," and he pointed to an old sword hanging in a conspicuous place on the wall.

"Yes, uncle, it is the sword of which every Middleton is so proud, 'The Sword of Bunker Hill.'"

"Yes, the sword your great-grandfather wore on that bloody day. He was among the last to leave the trench. A British soldier sprang over the works, and snatched at a flag. This sword found its way to his heart, and seizing the flag, your great-grandfather bore it back. Warren fell by his side.

Ever since, that sword has been a precious heirloom in the Middleton family, descending from eldest son to eldest son; but, Lawrence, the succession will now be broken."

Thus speaking, Mr. Middleton took down the sword and handed it to his astonished nephew, saying: "Take it, Lawrence, it is rightfully yours."

"But this sword should go to Edward," stammered Lawrence.

"Edward would despise it; he despises everything that savors of the North. I sometimes think he despises me for being of Northern birth. More than that, this sword took a human life in defence of the flag you love, the flag that I repudiate, that to me has become the symbol of tyranny. I no longer have a right to it. Take it, Lawrence, I know you will never dishonor it."

Sinking on one knee, Lawrence took the sword, and reverently pressed it to his lips, then, in a voice trembling with emotion, said: "Uncle, may my right arm be palsied, if ever this sword is tarnished by a single act of mine."

"I have faith in you, that it never will be," said his uncle, "otherwise, I would break it in twain and throw it away."

Of all the gifts his uncle could give him, Lawrence felt he had received the one he would value the most.

"Now, uncle, I must bid you farewell," he said.

"I never can forget your kindness. Perhaps in time Edward will see differently, but until he does, I cannot even visit you."

"If war really come," said Mr. Middleton, "my home will be desolate, for Edward will be in it, nothing can keep him out of it. No, Lawrence, much as I hate to say so, as long as he is at home, you had better not visit us; but surely I shall see you; that is, if you do not go off to war. One thing more, Lawrence, if you are ever in trouble or in need, let me know. Neither will I now send you forth penniless."

Going to a small safe which stood in the room, he counted out five hundred dollars. "Here, Lawrence," said he, "take this for your present needs."

"Uncle, this after I have nearly broken your heart in doing as I have done?" cried Lawrence. "I cannot take it, you have already done too much."

"Lawrence, if you love me, as you say you do, take it. Don't make it harder for me than it is."

Lawrence took the money; he tried to thank his uncle, but his heart was too full. With bowed head, he went out of the room, and with him he carried that priceless gift, the Sword of Bunker Hill.

CHAPTER XII

A VALUABLE ALLY

FROM his interview with his uncle, Lawrence went directly to his room, finished packing, and soon was ready to leave the house. But one duty remained to be done — the hardest of all — that of bidding farewell to his Aunt Clara. He met his cousin Edward just coming out of his mother's room. He passed Lawrence with head high in air, and without speaking, but there was a look of triumph on his face which plainly said: " Go, you Yankee beggar, and never come back!"

As Lawrence entered his aunt's room, she arose to meet him, but he felt that her usual warmth was lacking. Her face was tear-stained, and Lawrence saw she had been weeping bitterly.

"I see that Edward has been here," said Lawrence, "has he told you all?"

"He told me that he and you had quarrelled, that there was bitter hate between you, and that you must leave the house at once, never to enter it again, or he would. Oh, Lawrence! Lawrence! what have you done thus to quarrel with my only son? It is a poor requital you have given me, for I have loved you almost as if you had been my own child."

"Aunt Clara," cried Lawrence chokingly, "don't

upbraid me; don't make my going harder than it is. I have come to bid you good-bye, never to enter this house again until Edward feels differently. You have been a mother to me; you have given me your love, and now you think me an ingrate. As God is my witness, Aunt Clara, I never loved this household better than I do now that I am about to leave it; I have never felt more grateful to you all, for what you have done for me."

"Why did you quarrel with Edward then?" sobbed his aunt.

"There is nothing personal between Edward and me. It is this miserable secession business. He is very angry because I am for the Union, and have joined a company of Home Guards."

"Why do you go with the North and against the South?" asked his aunt. "Your uncle is of Northern birth, like you, and yet he is for the South."

"Can you control the beating of your own heart, Aunt Clara? Can you by saying, ' I love the North and hate the South,' make it so? No; you love the South, you believe it is right, and you can no more help it than you can help breathing. I love the Union, believe in it, think that secession is not only wicked, but ruinous to the South. The flag of my country is dearer to me than life. I must be true to it, even if those I love turn against me."

"Do you think there will be war?" asked his aunt in a trembling voice.

"Yes, and, dear aunt, prepare yourself for a greater trial than has yet come. There will be war, and Edward will be one of the first to enlist."

"Oh no, no; I cannot have it," cried his aunt, "I cannot give my only son, even to my country."

"Nothing can keep him from it," said Lawrence, "not even your love. I know his nature; he is brave, impetuous. He already belongs to the Minute Men; his associates are Duke, Green, and others as young and impetuous as he. These Minute Men have sworn to take Missouri out of the Union; they will do it if they can."

"And you, what will you do?" asked his aunt.

"I have, as I told you, already joined a company of Home Guards. I shall fight for the Union."

"Fight for the Union, and against Edward?" gasped his aunt.

"Yes; but this I promise, if I ever meet him on the field of battle, no harm will come to him if I can help it. I will not raise a hand against him; no, not even to save my own life."

"Thank God for that!" sobbed his aunt. "But Lawrence, if war should come, why should you or Edward go? It would be like brother against brother."

"And that is what it will be in thousands of cases, brother against brother," replied Lawrence.

"If war come, the North, and the North alone, must answer to God," exclaimed his aunt. "As for you, Lawrence, may you be forgiven for raising your hand against those who love you. It is wise that you should go. If you remained I should feel as if we had an enemy in the household; but my prayers will go with you, that you may be protected, and come to see the great error you are committing."

Lawrence reverently raised the hand of his aunt to his lips and kissed it. Tears blinded his eyes, and without a word, he turned and left the house which had sheltered him for four years; left those who had taken him in when homeless and starving, those who had loved and cared for him. Once he faltered, turned, and looked back. He almost regretted his decision. How could he leave them, they thinking they had cherished an ingrate? Oh! it was bitter, bitter.

He raised his eyes, and over the court-house, he saw the Stars and Stripes flying. Could he aid in pulling that flag down? No, never. He turned from the house, and with resolute footsteps went on. He was once more homeless in St. Louis, but not penniless or friendless. Neither was he a helpless child. He had nearly the stature of a man; he was stronger than most men, and he had a stout heart.

The first thing to do was to look up a suitable room and boarding-place. This was not hard to find. He sent a drayman for his trunk, put his room to rights, and felt himself at home. The Sword of Bunker Hill he hung over the head of his bed. "So it will look down upon me," he said, "the first thing on which my eyes will rest when I open them in the morning."

It was late in the afternoon, before he had everything fixed to his satisfaction. The little room that he had rented bore little comparison to the magnificent chamber he had occupied at his uncle's. But now that was all past. He cared little for the luxury he had left, but the loss of their love, their respect — that left a wound in the heart that would take a long time to heal.

The company of which he had been elected an officer was to meet that evening. Here he would meet those who believed as he did, who were fighting to uphold the same principles which he upheld. There at least he would be among friends.

Before going to the drill he thought he would take a short walk. He met many he knew, but to his surprise, few returned his salutations. They simply returned his salute with a stony stare. He now realized for the first time that he was an outcast from the society in which he had moved. He was no longer the favorite nephew of the rich Mr. Middleton; he had been driven from his home, disgraced, scorned. Edward had lost no time during the day in reporting what had befallen Lawrence. All of the Minute Men knew it; it was the theme of conversation in every aristocratic home. Lawrence keenly felt these rebuffs. He would be insulted no more. Hereafter he would notice only those of his acquaintances who first noticed him. So with head erect, and step as proud as ever he walked on.

Coming to a small park, he sat down to think over the events of the day. Here one of the boys who attended the academy found him. His name was Guilford Craig, and he was the step-brother of Benton Shelley. He was a frail, sickly youth, and Lawrence had first won his friendship by defending him against the aggression of a much larger and stronger boy. His step-brother also domineered over him in a very insulting manner.

On the day that Lawrence had knocked down Shelley for calling him a coward, Guilford watched his chance, and coming up to Lawrence when no one was near, grasped his hand, and said: "I want to thank you for whipping Bent. I wished you had half killed him. I hate him. I tell you, I hate him."

Lawrence had thought it best not to pry too closely into a closet which concealed a family skeleton; so he said little, but watched Guilford. He saw that he always wore a kind of hunted look, and seldom took part in the boyish sports of the students; also that he was of a very secretive nature.

"I have been looking for you," said Guilford; "in fact, I followed you here. I saw those fellows cutting you, and I know what it was for: it was because you are for the Union," and sinking his voice to a whisper, " I am for the Union, too, but nobody knows it."

"You," answered Lawrence in surprise. "I thought you were a strong Southern boy, you always talked that way."

"I know that; I do it to fool them. You knew my step-brother, Bent, is one of the Minute Men. He is also in the Militia on General Frost's staff. General Frost often comes to the house, and I hear them talk. I learn lots of things. Father and my stepmother are both strong for the South. I have been trying to join the Minute Men. They say I am too young and weakly, but I will come it yet. Do you know what I am going to be?"

" No, what are you going to be? A general?" asked Lawrence.

"Will you never tell?"

"Not if you don't want me to."

"Will you swear on your honor?"

" If you want me to, yes."

The boy put his lips close to Lawrence's ear and whispered, " I am going to be a spy."

Lawrence started. The word " spy " had a hateful sound. It meant deceit, falsehood. But then he remembered that every general employed spies in war. It was a commander's business to find out all he could about the enemy.

"A spy, Guilford? That's dangerous business," answered Lawrence. "What put that in your head?"

"Oh! I have been reading a book about a spy; it's just grand. And then, I want to do the South all the damage I can. I hate slavery. I know something now which Frank Blair would like to know."

"Tell me," said Lawrence.

"Not without you will swear to tell no one who told you."

"Must I not tell Blair?"

"No, not Blair, or any other living soul. I will be your spy, on that condition. If you don't swear, I will tell no one, and you will be sorry."

Lawrence thought it was a queer condition for the boy to make, and regarded it as a boyish fancy; but it would do no hurt to promise, so he made the promise, and made it as strong as Guilford demanded.

"First," said Guilford, "I will tell you why I hate slavery, why I hate my step-brother, why I hate all of them.

"My mother died when I was a babe. Hannah, one of my father's slaves, became my black mammy. From her breast I drew the nourishment which kept me alive. How that black woman grew to love me! I was weak and sickly, and night after night she watched over me as tenderly as my own mother could have done. I grew to love her with all my heart. When I was six years of age, my father married again, a widow with one child, a boy three years older than myself. That boy is my step-brother, Benton Shelley. Hardly had he become an inmate of the house before he began to domineer over me. My father, immersed in business, paid little attention, and both my step-mother and Bent were very careful to be kind to me when my father was around. When he was away, I suffered martyrdom.

"Hannah saw it all, and her blood boiled, but she could do nothing. One day I did something Bent did n't like, and he struck me, struck me a cruel blow. Hannah saw it, and forgetting she was a slave, caught him, and gave him a good shaking.

"'Don't you ebber tich my bressed honey agin,' she cried, 'if you do, I tak yo' hide off,' and taking me sobbing and crying to her motherly bosom, she comforted me.

"Of course there was an uproar. My step-mother demanded that Hannah should be whipped, and then sold South. Father demurred at first, but at last for the sake of peace, he consented. And my step-mother, that she-devil, forced me to see Hannah whipped. Young as I was I was a fury. I flew at the officer who was to whip her, and was borne struggling and screaming away. I pleaded as only a child can plead, but it did no good. I could only cover my face with my hands, and refuse to look, but I heard the swish of the whip, and Bent cry,

'Harder! harder! Giver it to her harder.' How I have hated him ever since!

"During her punishment Hannah never uttered a groan or made a sound. Her heart seemed to have been broken. They sold her South, refusing to let me see her. The first night out, watching her opportunity, she threw herself overboard. Do you wonder I hate slavery?"

"No, I do not," replied Lawrence, deeply moved by the recital. "I, too, have suffered from slavery, suffered more than you know, yet the greatest kindness I ever received has been from those who owned slaves."

"I think," continued Guilford, "that the whipping of Hannah changed my whole nature. I became secretive, and my only thought was for revenge. As I grew older, I rebelled against Bent's domineering ways. He never struck me but once again, and then I sprang at him with a knife, and would have killed him, if one of the servants had not held me. I told him if he ever struck me again, I would kill him, if I had to do it in his sleep. Since that time he has not dared to touch me. My stepmother also uses me with some semblance of kindness, but I know both she and Bent would rejoice if I were out of the way, for then they would inherit the property. You know father is very wealthy."

"Has your father no children by your stepmother?" asked Lawrence.

"Yes, two little girls, and I love them dearly. I know they think more of me than they do of Bent. His way is rougher with them."

"How about this spy business?"

"That is what I am going to tell you. Father and George talk very openly before me, for they believe I am a greater fire-eater than even Bent. You ought to hear me hurrah for Jeff Davis, and curse the Yankees!"

Lawrence shivered at such duplicity, but thought it wise to say nothing, and Guilford continued.

"When General Frost is there, they frequently hold secret consultations in the library, to which I am not admitted. But there is a closet off the library, and I hide in that, and hear every word that is said. What I want to see you for this evening is to tell you that they are after the United States arsenal."

"Yes, we all know that, but they will have to fight to get it," replied Lawrence.

"Don't be too sure. Major Bell has entered into a secret agreement with Frost to surrender the arsenal to him without firing a shot."

"Great Heavens! can that be so?" ejaculated Lawrence. "Is there not some mistake?"

"There is no mistake. I heard Frost say so."

"Blair must know of this at once. May I not tell him my source of information?"

"Never! Remember your oath; a word as to

whom you received this information from, and you get no more," exclaimed Guilford, with vehemence.

Lawrence saw it was no use to urge him further, so he said: "Do you know I have left my uncle's house, driven out because I am for the Union?"

"Yes, all the boys know it. Bent fairly danced for joy when he heard it."

" I have now secured a room at No.—, ——Street. When you have any information to give, you can find me there. But I must see Blair; also, it is time to go to drill. Try and see me to-morrow. I will then know just what to tell you."

Lawrence was already late, and the drill was in progress when he arrived at the headquarters of his company. The news of his expulsion from his uncle's house had reached them, and more than one asylum was offered him. Carl Mayer begged that he make his father's house his home, but Lawrence told them he had already secured quarters, but thanked them all heartily for their kindness.

Just as the drill was closing, Frank Blair, accompanied by a few other prominent Union men of the city, came in. As soon as he had an opportunity Lawrence said he would like to see him in private, as he had something important to communicate.

"How about the gentlemen with me?" asked Blair.

"They can come too," said Lawrence, "for I want advice."

The party repaired to a private room, and there Lawrence told his story.

"I am not surprised at Major Bell, except for one thing," said Blair. "I have always considered him a traitor at heart, and that he would surrender the arsenal at the first demand. But that he would enter into a secret pledge to do so, before any demand was made on him, is almost past belief. But it is only what the traitors are doing all over the country, holding onto the offices only to betray the Government they have sworn to support. You consider your information perfectly reliable, do you, Lieutenant Middleton?"

"Perfectly. I will stake my reputation on it," replied Lawrence.

"Yet I should feel safer if I knew who was your informant," said Blair. "We have to meet duplicity and falsehood on every side."

"I would gladly tell you, if I could," said Lawrence, "but as I explained, my informant is adamant on that point. I and I alone must know who he is."

"I think," said Mr. Glover, one of the gentlemen present, "that it is well to let the matter rest as it is. We all have confidence in Lieutenant Middleton; and, if as he says, his informant has access to the secret counsels of the enemy, it is highly important that we do not cut off the source of that information."

"Then you think it right that I should encourage

my informant in his deception? I confess I have
had my doubts. It — it don't look right."

At this they all laughed heartily. "My boy,"
said Blair, "have you not heard the old adage, that
the only way to fight the devil is with fire? How
can we know the plots of such perjured traitors as
Major Bell, unless by just such means as you are
employing? Encourage your informant all you can;
get all the information out of him possible. Now to
your private affairs, Lieutenant; I hear your uncle
has cast you out."

"Yes, I left the house this morning, never to
enter it again unless I am invited."

"I hardly thought that of your uncle," replied
Blair. "He always seemed to me a very fair, conservative man. I had hopes he would be with us."

"He never would have done it," said Lawrence,
"if it had not been for my cousin Edward. Uncle
had to choose between him and me. Edward declared he would never enter the house again if I
stayed."

"Ah!" said Blair, "that makes a difference.
Edward Middleton is with Basil Duke, Green, and
others. We shall have trouble with those young
fellows before we are through with them. They
are a daring set. But now, Lieutenant, that you
are out of a home, what are your plans for the
future?"

"I have made none as yet, except to engage a

room and board; I must look around a little," replied Lawrence.

"What do you say to becoming my orderly and confidential clerk? I have no doubt that war will come, and come soon. In that case, the regiments we now are forming will be mustered into the United States service, and I will see that you hold your present position. Until that time consider yourself in my pay."

"I gladly accept your proposition, Mr. Blair," said Lawrence; "and you do me great honor in offering it."

Blair and other Union men of St. Louis lost no time in informing General Scott, at Washington, of Major Bell's contemplated treachery. He was promptly removed, and Major Peter V. Hagner appointed in his place.

CHAPTER XIII

NATHANIEL LYON

IN St. Louis was the largest arsenal in the United States. It contained sixty thousand stands of arms, and an immense quantity of munitions of war. One of the first acts of the rebellious States was to seize the Government arsenals within their borders, under the absurd claim that all property of the National Government belonged to the State in which the property was situated.

From the very inception of the rebellion, the Confederates had their eyes fixed on the St. Louis arsenal. If they had that, they would control most of the arms of the Federal Government in the West. It would place the Mississippi Valley at their mercy, and we have seen how early the Missouri secessionists laid plans to capture it.

At the time Major Bell was secretly plotting with General Frost to surrender the arsenal, but few States had seceded. Major Bell posed as a loyal citizen of the United States. It was this secret treason with which the Federal Government had to deal at every turn, and which came so near being successful in dragging the border States into rebellion.

To guard this great arsenal there were but sixty

soldiers, and these in command of an officer plotting treason. In January the Government sent forty more soldiers to help to guard the arsenal. If the forty had been forty thousand they would not have created greater excitement. The papers issued extras, denouncing the outrage. The great State of Missouri had been insulted. If the arsenal was in danger, they would guard it. Excited throngs paraded the streets; fiery speeches were made. It looked at one time as if the coming of these forty soldiers would create a riot.

The military division of the West contained most of the territory between the Mississippi River and the Rocky Mountains, and was under the command of General William S. Harney, with headquarters at St. Louis. He was a brave and skilful officer, but of advanced age, and also of Southern birth and a slave-owner. For these reasons he was distrusted by the Union men, and not without cause. A Southern writer says of him: " While he sympathized with the South, he loved the Union and knew no other country, and was absolutely loyal to the flag."

This may be true, but it is also true that his sympathy for the South was so great, and the thought of shedding the blood of his friends so terrible, that he would have let St. Louis and Missouri drift into the Confederacy, without firing a gun to prevent it. The situation in St. Louis needed not only a man who loved the flag, but a man quick to act, fearless; one who would not be tied by red tape; one who would dare and do things, even to the disobeying of his superiors.

Early in February, such a man came to St. Louis in the person of Captain Nathaniel Lyon, who had been ordered with his company from Fort Riley, Kansas. In Lyon, Frank Blair found a man after his own heart. Lyon was described at that time as being a man about forty-three years of age, of less than medium height, slender and angular, with abundant hair of a sandy color, and a reddish-brown beard. He had deep-set blue eyes; and his features were rough and weather-beaten. No humble captain ever made history more rapidly for a few months than he. He took in the situation at a glance, and at once set to work to save St. Louis and Missouri to the Union. He and Blair worked hand in hand; between them there was complete agreement.

Blair already had the nucleus of an army in his regiments of Home Guards. Lyon met them, drilled them, infused into them the spirit of soldiers; but they were soldiers without arms.

To a soldier like Lyon, the safety of the arsenal was the first object sought. He was very much dissatisfied with the preparations which Major Hagner had made for defending it, which in reality was no preparation at all. Lyon claimed that he outranked Major Hagner and should have supreme command in St. Louis. This Hagner refused; the dispute was referred to Washington, and Hagner was upheld. At last Lyon was given command of the troops in St. Louis, but Major Hagner was left in control of the ordnance stores. This tied Lyon's hands, as far as the arms were concerned.

Lawrence was introduced to Lyon soon after the latter's arrival, and the story told of his getting at the most secret machinations of the Rebels.

"Who is your informant?" asked Lyon.

"That I am not at liberty to tell," answered Lawrence.

The reply nettled Lyon. "I have little use for information of which I do not know the source," he bluntly replied.

Lawrence drew himself proudly up. "You can consider me the source, Captain. If I ever mislead you, hang me. This is all I have to say. If you wish any information from me hereafter, let me know. Good-day, sir." And Lawrence walked away, as if he, not Lyon, were in command.

Lyon looked after him, not in anger, but admiringly. "Who is that boy?" he asked of Blair. "He seems to have the right sort of stuff in him."

"He is my confidential secretary," answered Blair, "and a lieutenant in one of my companies of Home Guards."

Blair then gave Lyon a full history of Lawrence as far as he knew it. But Blair did not know of

Lawrence's experiences in Missouri and Kansas, and how his father had met his death.

"And so he was kicked out of one of the richest homes in the city on account of his loyalty to the flag?" said Lyon.

"Yes, and I have found him true as steel," answered Blair. "Why he cannot tell the source of his information, he explained to me: the moment he tells, he gets no more information. I will vouch for him. So far I have found the information he gives me absolutely correct."

"It 's all right, if you say so, Blair. I like the spirit the boy shows. Let me see him again."

Lawrence was summoned. Lyon apologized for his bluntness, but excused himself by saying he found so much double-dealing in St. Louis he hardly knew whom to trust. "Bring me all the information you can, Lieutenant, it will be gladly received," he said, as he closed the interview.

And from that day, the relations of Lawrence and Lyon grew closer and closer.

CHAPTER XIV

THE FOURTH OF MARCH

HOW many of our young readers are aware that the war for the preservation of the Union barely escaped commencing on the fourth of March, the very day that Lincoln was inaugurated President, instead of the twelfth of April, by the bombardment of Fort Sumter? Yet such is the case, and history came nearly being written much differently. That the streets of St. Louis did not run red with blood, at the very moment Lincoln was making his inauguration speech, was entirely owing to the fact that Frank Blair and Lyon had been forewarned, and did all in their power to prevent it. That the great Rebellion was not precipitated before Lincoln had taken his oath of office seems almost like a special dispensation of Providence; but it was owing to the information placed in the hands of Lawrence by Guilford Craig, that the whole plot was laid bare.

Lawrence and Guilford had met two or three times by secret appointment, when Guilford told him that even their meetings might be dangerous, for the spies of the Minute Men were everywhere; so they resolved to establish a secret postoffice.

Near where Lawrence boarded was an old brick

wall, badly cracked. The place was dark and secluded. Behind in one of these cracks, large enough for a hand to be inserted, they resolved to establish their office, but not *in* the crack, for papers might be seen. Lawrence carefully removed one of the bricks next to the crack, then he removed the brick behind that. He now carefully replaced the first brick removed, and this left a receptacle behind it the size of a brick, which could be reached by inserting the hand in the crack. It made a safe and secure hiding-place, and in it were placed secrets which confounded all the machinations of the plotters.

The first information that Lawrence carried to Blair and Lyon was important, yet it puzzled them to understand exactly what it meant. It was to the import that the Minute Men had rented the Berthold mansion at the corner of Fifth and Pine Streets, and were converting it into a fort. The most improved arms had been transported into the building, boxed as household goods. Even a cannon had been smuggled in that way.

"I have not yet been able to learn what it all means," wrote Guilford, "but I reckon I shall soon, for they have promised to admit me as one of the Minute Men. As soon as I am a member, I will take care to learn all their secrets. General Frost was here last evening, and whatever they were planning, I am sure he is in it. I had company, and so was unable to occupy my secret hiding-place in the closet."

"This converting the Berthold mansion into a fort means mischief of some kind," said Blair to Lyon; "we shall have to watch it closely."

"I have had my spies watch the mansion," said Lyon, "and I find that the information imparted by Lieutenant Middleton is absolutely correct. It is wonderful how he gets it. Every door is guarded by sentinels, and no one is admitted without the password. I wonder what the next move will be."

General Lyon had not long to wait. On the night of the second of March, Lawrence found a very important communication in the secret receptacle. It was a communication which set every drop of blood in his veins tingling, and he lost no time in communicating its contents to Blair and Lyon. Guilford had succeeded in joining the Minute Men. He now had free access to the Berthold mansion, and had learned all their plans. It was a gigantic conspiracy, in which Governor Jackson, General Frost, and the Minute Men were all concerned. The conspiracy was to culminate March the fourth, the day Lincoln was to be inaugurated as President. They wanted some excuse to attack and capture the arsenal. As the State had not seceded, and as Jackson and Frost still professed allegiance to the United States flag, they durst not attack it outright. Therefore on the fourth of March, the mansion was to be fully garrisoned, and the Confederate flag hoisted over it. This they fully believed would create a bloody riot. The Minute Men were confident they could hold the house against any force that Blair or Lyon could bring against it, unless they had artillery. While the riot, as it would be called, was raging around the Berthold mansion, General Frost, under the pretence of quelling the riot, was to march, with his militia and numerous companies of Minute Men which had been formed throughout the city, to the arsenal, capture it, and then if need be, turn their guns on the mob in the street. All this under the pretext of keeping the peace.

Numerous Minute Men were also detailed to go through the crowd, exciting them to deeds of violence, and urging them to attack the Berthold mansion, and pull down the "dirty rag," if the mob seemed a little backward in attacking the place. It was a black, a hellish conspiracy, and if carried out, successful or unsuccessful, it would have made the streets of St. Louis shambles.

"My God! what will they do next?" exclaimed Blair, as Lawrence laid this information before him.

Lyon's stern face grew sterner. "And here I am," he exclaimed passionately, "bound hand and foot. Not a single gun can I have from that arsenal to help to defend it. All I can rely on is my few soldiers."

"There must be no riot," declared Blair, bringing his first down on the table with great force. "We must prevent it. We shall have to let that rag float."

"How can we prevent it?" asked Lyon; "mobs are hard to control."

"By warning our men, by telling them on no account must they bring on a conflict."

The third of March was a busy day with Blair and his lieutenants. Only a few were let into the real secret, but every Union man was warned not to bring on a conflict on the morrow. It made no difference, they were told, what the provocation was, how vile the epithets that might be hurled upon them, their tongues must be silent, their hands be restrained. It was the day Lincoln was to be inaugurated; there must be no bloodshed to cloud the beginning of his presidency, or to make his task more difficult.

But Blair had his Home Guards gather at their halls, where they were to remain quiet but ready for any emergency. If orders came, they were not to go to quell any riot which might be raging in the streets, but march to the defence of the arsenal, and stand by it to the last man.

"If the arsenal be attacked," said Lyon to Blair, "I will arm your men who come to defend it, if I have to kill Hagner to get the guns. I will take the consequences afterwards."

When the Home Guards met to drill that night,

all the officers were impressed with the importance of controlling themselves and their men on the morrow; that on no account must they bring on a conflict.

In the meantime there was high glee in the ranks of the conspirators. So far everything had worked to their satisfaction. The Berthold mansion had been fully armed. It would be garrisoned by between one and two hundred desperate young men, all that could be successfully handled in the house; there were two or three rifles to every man. A double-shotted cannon guarded the entrance. There would be hundreds of their friends on the outside, to stir up strife, and then to help them when the attack came. At the first sound of fighting, Frost, and the companies of Minute Men throughout the city, were to march on the arsenal. As far as they could see, their plans were unknown; the Union men had not taken the alarm. On the morrow Lincoln might be made President, but St. Louis and Missouri would be safe in the arms of the Confederacy.

To the Union men who knew of the plot there was little sleep that night. As for Lyon, he was like a caged wild beast. To be tied hand and foot by the red tape of the War Department; to be surrounded by traitors, and not allowed to lift a hand, was the situation of Lyon, on this night of March the third. But on this he was resolved — to defend the arsenal to the last man.

Those who plotted rebellion in St. Louis had only to look across the river to see the free State of Illinois. There on this fourth of March, 1861, all was rejoicing. There the flag of the Union was floating, unfettered and beloved. In that State, this day was a joyful one, for was not one of her sons to become President of the United States — a son whose name is to live forever in history?

So on this day, the people of Illinois rejoiced, all unmindful of the war clouds gathering just across the river. And with Illinois the whole North rejoiced. The great majority of its people still slumbered on in fancied security. Although the President of their choice had to creep through Baltimore like a criminal, they cherished the thought that in some way, when Lincoln became President, the dark clouds would be swept away, and there would be no war. So they slumbered on, until the thunder of Sumter's guns awoke them. Little did the nation think how near the awakening came on this, the fourth of March.

St. Louis passed a feverish night. Thousands of its citizens swore that Lincoln should never be President of Missouri. They turned with longing eyes to the newly arisen star of the Southern Confederacy. In the darkness of the night, the enemies of the Republic were busy. When the morning sun arose, and the citizens of St. Louis looked at the dome of their Court-house, over which the Stars and Stripes were wont to wave, the flag was not there. In its place waved the flag of the State of Missouri. Those who first saw could scarcely believe their eyes; they looked and looked again, but there was no mistake, the State flag and that alone met their gaze. Instinctively they turned toward the Berthold mansion, and there proudly floating above it, was the flag of the newly born Confederacy; at every window stood men with guns; and from the open portal frowned a cannon.

As if borne on the wings of the wind, the news flew that the city was in open revolt, that the Confederate flag had been raised, and that the city was in the hands of the enemies of the Federal Government.

An excited throng began to gather. The flag was greeted with wild cheering by the Southerners, with groans and curses by those who loved the Union. Soon from the Court-house the State Flag was lowered; in its place arose the banner of freedom; and as the breeze caught its folds, and the rays of the sun gilded each star, there burst forth a mighty cheer from the crowd, but only to be followed by the sullen roar of groans and curses, and wild hurrahs for Jeff Davis and the Southern Confederacy.

But over the Berthold mansion there still floated the flag of treason. Larger and more excited grew the mob that thronged around it. Thousands blocked the streets. Around the house the mob surged and roared like the billows of an angry sea. With heavy clubs the police charged the mob, but they might as well have tried to stem the tide of Niagara's mighty flood. From the inmates of the house there came taunts, jeers, and vile epithets, almost too brutal to be borne.

" Why don't you come and take down the flag?" they shouted from doors and windows. " Where are Frank Blair and his Dutch?"

Oh! yes; where were Frank Blair and his German Home Guards? Had they proven craven at the last moment? Thousands looked at that flag, and shook their fists, and cursed and swore, and wondered why Blair and his Guards did not come to haul it down.

Thousands of others looked, and shouted encouragement to those within. " Keep her a-flying, boys," they shouted. " We will help you." "Down with Abe Lincoln!" " Down with Frank Blair and his Dutch minions!" " Hurrah for Jeff Davis!" And from the house there still poured the revilings meant to incite the mob to frenzy.

The excitement spread throughout the entire city. It was a city in which pandemonium reigned. White-faced women looked from the windows, and wrung their hands in agony. Rumors flew thick and fast: The Confederates had the city in their power; they had the arsenal. No, Blair was marching on the Berthold mansion with his Home Guards. The streets would run red with blood. And they strained their ears to catch the first sound of combat.

As the hours passed, the mob grew. Why did not Frank Blair and his Home Guards come? Hundreds were in favor of storming the house.

"Why don't you come and get the flag, cowards, cravens, nigger-worshippers?" was shouted down at the mob.

Stung to frenzy, a few young men made a rush for the door; they were without weapons, but had strong arms. At their head was Carl Mayer. They were met and flung back. They were preparing for another dash when Lawrence rushed to Carl's side.

"Carl, Carl," he cried, "What are you doing? Have you forgotten your orders? For the love of Heaven, don't bring on a conflict."

"I can't bear it," cried Carl, "I will show them we are not all cowards."

"You must bear it; we all must bear it. Our time has not come yet."

In the door of the house stood Benton Shelley. He saw Lawrence and shook his sword at him. "Come on, coward, ingrate! you who have turned against those who fed and clothed you," he cried. "Come on, if you have a drop of red blood in your black veins!"

At a window above stood his cousin Edward, who scowled on him but said nothing. At another window he saw Guilford Craig with a gun in his hands. The boy saw him, laid a finger on his lips, and then began to shout down the vilest of epithets on the Yankees and the Dutch.

How could the boy play such a double part? It was an enigma Lawrence could not solve. But were not the Confederates playing the same kind of a part? Was not General Frost the personification of deceit and treachery?

Inside of the Berthold mansion, the leaders of the plot raved and stormed. Duke, and Green, and Quinlan, and Champion, and McCoy were beside themselves. Why did not Blair come with his Home Guards? Why did he not storm their citadel? They were prepared, if need were, to give their lives for the cause they loved. They were not only brave, but desperate. If Governor Jackson had only said the word, they would have charged the mob and stormed the arsenal, regardless of consequences. Many of those boys in the Berthold mansion gave their lives, afterwards, to the South; others rose to high rank in the Confederate army.

As Blair and his Home Guards did not appear, the fury of the mob gradually spent itself. Unarmed men could not attack a stronghold like the Berthold mansion, and when night came, the danger was over; but above the mansion, the Confederate flag still floated, and there it remained for many a day. Many a loyal heart in St. Louis that night, was sick and faint. They believed that Blair, when the crisis came, had failed; but those who knew and understood, rejoiced that, for the time being, the danger had passed.

As for the conspirators, they were both elated and depressed; depressed because their plans had failed; elated because they believed it was cowardice on the part of the Home Guards that prevented Blair from attacking them.

But they were to find out their mistake later; they were to meet Blair's regiment on the bloody field of Wilson Creek.

CHAPTER XV

A DREAM OF EMPIRE

O N the very day that the convention, elected by the people to consider the status of Missouri in the Union, met in Jefferson City, Luther Glenn of Georgia arrived in the city. He was sent as a representative of the Confederate States, to try to induce Missouri to secede, and was received with open arms by Governor Jackson.

Although not a single secessionist had been elected to that convention, the Governor did not for a moment cease his efforts to drag the State into open rebellion. He certainly showed courage worthy of a better cause. Introducing Mr. Glenn to an immense audience which had gathered in the street, he made a fiery speech, defying the members of the convention, saying that the place for Missouri was in the Southern Confederacy, and that he would do all in his power to place her there. "And there is where she will be before many days," he cried.

No doubt when he spoke these words, he believed that the plot about to be sprung in St. Louis would be successful, and that the city and arsenal would soon be in the hands of Frost. So tyrannical were the methods of the Governor and the rampant secessionists who flocked to Jefferson City, that the convention was forced to adjourn and to meet in St. Louis, where it could deliberate in peace. Mr. Glenn, the Southern Commissioner, was feasted and toasted in Jefferson City, and made much of by the Governor and the Legislature. When the St. Louis plot failed, the Governor was greatly disappointed, but he relaxed none of his efforts to force the State out of the Union.

To this end a secret meeting was held at the Governor's mansion, to which several hesitating members of the Legislature were invited. They were to meet Mr. Glenn, and he was to explain to them what the Confederacy hoped to accomplish, and why it would be suicidal in Missouri not to break away from the old Union.

" In the first place," said Mr. Glenn, " you must understand the South is out to stay. The North can offer us no compromise that we will accept. Lincoln must let us go in peace, or there will be war. If war comes, it is absurd to think that the North can conquer us. The Yankees may be good money-makers, but they will make poor fighters. The independence of the South is assured. This being the fact, does not the salvation, the future prosperity of the State depend on Missouri joining its sister slave States? Now, gentlemen, what are your objections, if you have any? "

" In the first place," spoke up one of the hesitating members, " the State has just voted by eighty thousand majority, to remain in the Union. If I understand the doctrine of State Rights, that vote should bind us."

"That vote would be reversed, should Lincoln attempt to coerce a single State," spoke up the Governor. "Sterling Price has been elected president of the convention. We have many friends among the delegates, who will be with us, if a single shot be fired against the South. Sterling Price has assured me he will be with us. He is for the Union if it can be preserved without bloodshed, not otherwise."

"The North may consent to let the cotton States go," said another member, "but I cannot see how they can consent to let Missouri and the other border slave States go. Look at the position of this State. It controls the upper Missouri; it controls the mouth of the Ohio; it eats right into the heart of the North; it is surrounded on three sides by free States, for the fight for Kansas is already lost. You may be assured the North will fight, before it gives up Missouri."

"Then let war come," shouted the fiery Vest. "I am ready and willing to follow Old Virginia wherever she may lead, and no one can doubt that she will go with the South. I defy the convention, I defy the submissionists, I will never submit to Northern rule."

This sentiment of Vest was wildly applauded.

"It seems to me," spoke up another, "that if we go to war, we shall lose the very thing for which we are contending — slavery. I have just read Lincoln's inaugural address, and I see that in it he solemnly assures the South that he has no intention of interfering with slavery where it is; that he will protect it in its constitutional rights. It is only the extension of slavery to which he is opposed. Now, if the South secedes does she not forever cut off all hope of the extension of slavery?"

"No," thundered Jackson, "Lincoln's proposition is to throttle slavery, choke it to death by slow degrees. Better have it die, and die at once."

"But," urged the objector, "I have heard that Lincoln has said that it would be better for the United States to buy every slave, and pay the market price, than have one year of war. That would make the South fabulously rich, and we would still have the negroes to work for us. If we go to war and win, slavery would still be hemmed in, even if we got the Territories west of us, for these Territories are barren wastes; but west of the Northern States are vast Territories. The North would grow richer and more powerful all the time, the South weaker and poorer."

"What has been said," replied Mr. Glenn, "only shows that some of you gentlemen little understand the aim and purposes of the South. I am here to tell you what they are. In the first place, the North would never consent to buy our slaves; in the second place, the South would never consent to sell. So that talk of Mr. Lincoln of buying our slaves is pure nonsense. Slavery is the chief corner-stone of the Confederacy. It is the only nation ever established that recognizes slavery as a divine institution, established by God, for the good of the world. It is written that Ham shall serve, and no laws of man can alter that divine decree. The South has been preparing for this for years. In fact, we rejoice that Lincoln was elected President. We split the National Democratic Convention for that very purpose. Our leaders have the future of the South all mapped out. Forces are now at work to bring it about.

" What if the North decides to let us go in peace — that the National Government has no right to coerce us? That establishes the right of secession. Any State can withdraw from the Union if it wishes. No State in the Confederacy will wish to secede, for slavery will be the chain which will bind us together, and to break a single link would be death. Not so with the North. You say it is richer and more powerful than the South. It will not long be so. Our friends in the North, and they are legion and powerful, are only waiting for the Southern Confederacy to be an assured fact, when they will form a Northwestern Confederacy. They are sick and tired of the domination of New England.

"If war be declared, the break will come quicker,

for we shall be successful, and the Northwest will refuse to bear its part of the burden of the war. The Pacific States will form a nation of their own. In fact, within ten years after the independence of the South is acknowledged, I look for the North to be divided into at least three, if not four, different nations. This result is sure to come. Therefore, instead of being strong, the North will be divided, and be weak, and the South can enforce any demand that it makes. We shall claim Kansas and all territory west of Kansas to the Rocky Mountains.

"That is not all. It is to the south of us that our empire really lies. We will take Cuba. We should have had it long ago, if it had not been for the fanatical North. It should be ours by right. Mexico rent by its continual revolutions, would fall an easy prey, and we would push our conquest clear down to the isthmus. We shall have an empire that would rival Rome in her palmiest day. To cultivate this vast domain, we would legalize the African slave trade, with humane provisions. The South will be the grandest, the greatest, the most glorious power of all the earth. Should not such a prospect fire the heart of every true Southerner? Can Missouri afford to sit back, and not have a part in it?

"That, gentlemen, is what the South has been dreaming of, working for, for years. The time has come for the dream to become a fact. The sun has arisen on the great Southern Confederacy; it will never set."

Those present had listened in breathless attention. They saw the vision in all its glory, and it swept them from their feet.

Let us thank God, it was a dream which has not been verified.

CHAPTER XVI

THE CALL TO ARMS

IF Basil Duke and Colton Green had had their way, when their plot to create a riot failed, they boldly would have stormed the arsenal; but they were held back by Governor Jackson. It was also doubtful, if they had stormed it, if they could have captured it, for it was now garrisoned by five hundred men.

For the part which Lawrence had played in the affair of the fourth, he received the heartiest commendation from both Blair and Lyon. "Lieutenant," said Lyon, "we owe you much, and when war comes, as it will come, I shall remember you. That spy of yours does his work well. I hope he will keep it up, but it is dangerous business."

"I saw him," said Lawrence, laughing, "among the Minute Men in the Berthold mansion. He was among the most active, and the way he handed down insulting epithets to us was a caution."

"If he keeps us as well posted as he has," said Blair, "they at least cannot take us by surprise."

Now came some weeks of intrigue, plot, and counter plot. While Duke and Green were away, the Minute Men were not so active; but Frost never lost

sight of the fact that he must have the arsenal.
What Lyon feared was a sudden and secret attack,
and that Hagner would give it up without a blow.
He pleaded with Hagner to strengthen the defences
of the arsenal; but this Hagner not only refused to
do, but refused to let Lyon do it. Both Hagner and
Harney declared that the arsenal was in no danger.
Lyon now averred that his commission as captain
in the regular army antedated Hagner's, and that
he should have supreme command. The quarrel was
taken to General Harney, and also to General Scott
at Washington, and both sustained Hagner. But
Blair and Lyon did not give up the fight. They
stormed Washington with petitions, and at last
received an order that Lyon might command the
troops, but Hagner should still control the arms and
munitions of war in the arsenal.

About this time there came another important
communication from Guilford Craig. It was to the
effect that Basil Duke and Colton Green had been
sent on a secret mission to Jefferson Davis, by Governor Jackson and General Frost. The object was
to secure cannon from the Confederacy to batter
down the walls of the arsenal, should it be found
necessary to take it by force. The communication
also stated that Frost was negotiating with captains
of steamboats to see if they would not secretly bring
cannon up on their boats, and at a given signal, open
fire on the arsenal.

All these things troubled Lyon, and made him doubly vigilant. Among the officers at the arsenal there were some whose loyalty was unquestioned, and on whom. Lyon could depend. Preëminent among these officers were Captains Sweeney and Saxton, and Lieutenant Lathrop. Lawrence will never forget the day that Lyon called these officers in consultation. Only Frank Blair and Lawrence were present with Lyon at the interview. Fixing his keen eyes on the officers, Lyon suddenly asked this startling question:

"If a mob surrounded the arsenal, as did a mob the Little Rock arsenal, and if the Governor demanded that the arsenal should be surrendered to him to prevent bloodshed, and Major Hagner should surrender it, what would you do?"

For full a minute, not a word was said. The three officers gazed at each other, and their faces grew pale. The silence became oppressive. Lyon sat with his eyes fixed upon them, as if he would read their very hearts.

At length Captain Sweeney slowly raised his hand toward heaven, and said slowly, but with terrible emphasis: "As God is my judge, I would shoot Hagner as a traitor, assume command, if no one else would, and defend the arsenal to the last."

"And I would do the same," echoed both Saxton and Lathrop.

A flame leaped into Lyon's eyes. "And I would

do the same!" he exclaimed. "If I knew I should be court-martialled and shot for the act."

Frank Blair gazed in admiration at the men. "With such officers as you, gentlemen, that arsenal can never be taken," he said; "and if the authorities in Washington can't see an inch beyond their noses, we will start a little rebellion of our own, if necessary."

Lawrence always remembered that scene as one of the most remarkable he witnessed during the war — subordinate officers swearing death to a superior, if he persisted in treason.

Suddenly a bomb-shell fell into the ranks of the Unionists. By secret intrigue, and false representations, that Blair and Lyon were doing the cause of the Union more hurt than good, an order came from the War Department for Lyon to go to Fort Leavenworth.

There was great rejoicing among the disloyal element when the order came. At that time Lincoln was handling the border States very carefully, in the hope that by hearkening to the so-called conservatives he might save the States to the Union. It was this conservatism which so angered General Nelson in Kentucky. Whether Lincoln's course was the wisest or not will never be known, but the fact remains that if it had not been for General Nelson in Kentucky, and Blair and Lyon in Missouri, both States would have been lost to the Union. It was no gloved affair with these men; they struck with an iron hand, and their boldness and courage saved those States from open rebellion.

With Lyon gone, nothing would prevent Hagner from giving up the arsenal, if he so willed. Frank Blair once more threw himself into the breach. What does not the nation owe to this man? He achieved victories by his firmness and boldness, as great as were ever won by Grant or Sherman on the field of battle. He at once repaired to Washington, and by his protests and representations, he induced General Scott to rescind his order transferring Lyon to Fort Leavenworth. Once more had the machinations of the conspirators failed. Lyon would still remain as the watchdog of the arsenal.

On April 12, the guns of Fort Sumter echoed and reëchoed through the land. The North awoke from its slumber. War had come; the Union could be preserved only by the sword. Throughout the South the firing on Sumter was received with the wildest demonstrations of joy; throughout the North with a grim determination that the Union must be preserved at all hazards.

In Missouri the call to arms was welcome to both sides. In fact the State had been in the throes of civil strife for months. Thousands of Union men had been driven from their homes. Governor Jackson, notwithstanding his loud protestations of preserving the peace, had done nothing to protect them.

St. Louis was already filling up with refugees fleeing from their homes, their only crime, that they loved the flag of their country. From the very first, the secessionists had begun the mobbing and lynching of Union men, and the civil authorities looked quietly on. Governor Jackson had a queer way of preserving the peace.

The Call to Arms caused the waverers to take sides. A man had to be for the Union or against it. The conditional Union men were swept out of existence. To President Lincoln's call for troops, Governor Jackson sent an insolent reply. "Not one man will Missouri furnish to coerce the South." It afterwards furnished over one hundred thousand. The declaration of war encouraged Governor Jackson and General Frost to renewed efforts to take the State out of the Union, and to capture the arsenal. All over the State, the secessionists became active; a reign of terror was beginning.

The day after Sumter fell, Lawrence met Guilford Craig on the street. Without appearing to notice him, Craig said: "You will find an important communication in the secret place to-night. But I wish to tell you something I dare not put on paper, for if the paper were found, it would tell who wrote it. I have been detailed as an orderly to General Frost. I have charge of his quarters. I have had a duplicate key to his desk made, and hereafter his secrets are my secrets."

He said no more, and sauntered on.   Never once had Craig looked toward Lawrence, as he was telling it.   Apparently they were strangers.   Lawrence looked after him in wonder.   What kind of a boy was this, who seemed to take delight in his duplicity?

Lawrence could hardly wait for the communication.   About midnight he found it, and taking it to the seclusion of his room, he read it.   Important it was, and early the next morning, he lost no time in carrying the communication to Blair and Lyon. These gentlemen read it through carefully, and Lyon smiled grimly as he said: "Forewarned is forearmed.   But what I should like to know is how your correspondent got hold of that private paper of Frost's.   It looks as if it were some one close to him."

Lawrence replied, "I should like to tell you, if I could; but I don't like to cut off the source of information."

"I should say not," said Lyon, "as long as the source keeps up."

The information sent was that General Frost had mapped out a course of procedure, that it had been submitted to Governor Jackson, who had fully endorsed it.   It was as follows:

First: Convene the General Assembly.

Second: Send an agent to the South to procure mortars and siege guns.

Third: Prevent the garrisoning of the Liberty arsenal.

Fourth: Warn the people that the calling out of troops by President Lincoln was illegal.

Fifth: Order me [Frost] to form a military camp near St. Louis.

Sixth: Order General Bowen to report to me [Frost].

General Bowen commanded the Missouri militia in the western part of the State, and Frost's object was to get as large a force of the militia to attack the arsenal as possible. What would have been the feelings of General Frost, if he had known that his secret plan was in the hands of Lyon, is not hard to imagine.

The Legislature before it adjourned had, in obedience to the wishes of the Governor, passed a law placing the police force of St. Louis in the hands of commissioners appointed by him. St. Louis had elected a Democratic Mayor in April. Thus the whole machinery of the city government was in the hands of the secessionists.

The hatred of the Southern element had become so intense against the Germans that a series of brutal assaults began, and in some cases murder was committed. The police winked at these outrages, and an arrest was seldom made. In turn, the Germans became greatly incensed, and threatened retaliation. It was with the utmost difficulty that Frank Blair and the officers of the Home Guards held them back.

One day word was brought to Lawrence that Ernest Kuenster, a young member of his company, had been caught by three Minute Men, and so brutally beaten that he lived but a short time; and that the neighborhood in which he lived was organizing for vengeance.

Lawrence hastened to the scene, and none too soon. The incensed Germans had caught two of the Minute Men, and were beating them to death. Lawrence arrived just as the men had been knocked down, and the crowd were about to jump upon them, and crush them beneath their heavy feet.

"Hold!" he cried in German, "hold, on your lives! These men must not be killed."

Most of the mob knew him, a number were members of his company. Among them was Carl Mayer.

"Carl, you in this!" cried Lawrence; "I am astonished. Now help me to pacify this gathering."

A hoarse growl went up from the mob; they did not wish to be balked of their prey. But the Germans, above all people, have learned obedience to law, and when the members of Lawrence's company heard one of their officers commanding them to keep order, they obeyed without hesitation. The mob were told to disperse, and the two young men assaulted were helped to their feet. To Lawrence's surprise, he saw that one of them was his cousin, and the other Randolph Hamilton, the brother of Dorothy Hamilton.

"Carl, you live close by," said Lawrence, "help me to get these two young men into your house, as soon as possible." Both the young men seemed dazed, and made no resistance. Once in the house, the blood was washed from their faces, and their wounds carefully dressed. Although both were much bruised, it was found that neither was seriously hurt.

"There, you are all right, old fellow," said Lawrence to Edward, after he had got him into shape, "but it is fortunate I came just as I did."

Edward had little to say. That Lawrence had saved his life, was a bitter pill for him to swallow; but young Hamilton was profuse in his thanks.

Lawrence found out that it was really his cousin who had started the mob, by snatching a flag from a German girl, and throwing it down, and trampling upon it; at the same time uttering some coarse remark.

After everything had been done for them that could be done, and they had somewhat recovered, Lawrence called a cab, and sent them home. At the parting, Edward gave Lawrence his hand, and a short "Thank you"; but Hamilton pressed him to call, so that his parents as well as himself might more fully thank him for his kindness.

There was excitement in both households on the arrival of the young men at their respective homes.

Edward told his story to his father and mother. "I suppose I did a very foolish thing," said Edward, "but when a Dutch huzzy shook a Yankee flag in my face, I snatched it from her, threw it down, and trampled upon it, and called her a vile name. I don't know where they all came from, but I had not walked twenty yards before we were surrounded by the mob, and it would have been all day with us, if Lawrence had not put in an appearance. I owe my life to him,— there is no denying it,— and I had rather be indebted to any one else."

"I don't see why," said his mother, "When Lawrence left, he told me he had nothing but love for you, and that if you two ever met on the battlefield, he would protect your life, even at the expense of his own."

"I can't understand it," said Edward, "the Union men don't seem to have any personal feeling in the matter; they say it is not individuals they are fighting, but in defence of the flag of their country. Now I hate every Yankee, hate them with an eternal hatred. That I should be indebted to Lawrence for my life, after I was the cause of his being turned out of this house, is humiliating to my pride. But if I ever meet him in battle, I will show him no Southern gentleman can be outdone in chivalry by a Yankee."

"Edward, you are altogether too hot-headed," said his father. "By your own account you insulted the girl. What if any one had bestowed such an epithet on your sister?"

"I would shoot him on sight; but these Dutch girls — "

"Their reputation is just as sacred to them as the reputation of our daughters is to us," said his father.

"I can't believe it," said Edward.

"There is where you make a mistake," answered Mr. Middleton. "You seem to think because you are a Southerner you are of a little finer clay than other people. And I am afraid the whole Southern people are making the same mistake. You despise the Yankees, and think they will not fight. Never was a greater mistake made. There is a long and bloody war before us. God only knows how it will end."

"I can't think it," said Edward; "we shall just eat the Yankees and Dutch up, when we get started."

His father sighed, and did not answer. He knew the North, and felt that the South was underrating the fighting qualities of its people. But after Edward went out, Mr. Middleton said to his wife, "Lawrence did just what I should have expected of him; there is noble blood in the boy."

In the Hamilton household also there was excitement, when Randolph appeared. He praised his deliverer without stint. "I always liked Lawrence Middleton," he added. "What a pity he turned Yankee!"

"Perhaps it was a good thing for you that he did turn Yankee," said his mother. "If he had not been with the Yankees, he could not have saved you."

"That's so," answered Randolph. "What do you think, sis?" addressing Dorothy. "Don't you think Lawrence is a fine fellow?" Now Randolph was a great favorite with Dorothy, and it distressed her beyond measure to see him all bruised up.

"I hate him," said Dorothy. "I saw him the other day, and told him never to speak to me again."

"Why, I thought he was a special favorite of yours," said Randolph. "If I mistake not, I have often heard you sing his praises."

"So I did, until he turned Yankee," pouted the girl, " and — and — "

"And what?" asked Randolph.

"He — he actually said to me that Lola Laselle is better looking than I am."

"Ha! ha! there is where the shoe pinches, is it," laughed Randolph. "But, sis, I agree with him;

and if Lola were a little older, I should have another grievance against young Middleton, beside being a Yankee. But how did he come to tell you Lola was better looking than you?"

"Oh! I met Lola, and cut her dead, because her folks are Union. Lawrence came across her crying, and he told her I had cut her on account of jealousy, because she was better looking."

"Served you right, sis, — better apologize to him the next time you meet him."

"What! apologize to a Yankee?" she asked, in surprise.

"Certainly. Did n't he save my life? Or don't that count?"

"Oh, Dolph," cried Dorothy throwing her arms around his neck, and kissing his bruised cheek, "I should have died if you had been killed. I will thank him, if I see him; but I hate him all the same."

"You and Ed Middleton would make a good team," said Randolph; "he hates everything that smells of Yankeedom."

The next day Lawrence happened to meet Dorothy on the street. He was somewhat surprised that instead of passing him with her head up, she stopped and held out her hand. "I hate you, Lawrence Middleton," she exclaimed, "but I want to thank you for saving Dolph from those horrid Dutch."

"Now that is real nice in you, since you told

me you would never speak to me again," replied Lawrence. "Now please quit hating me, and let us be good friends."

"Can't do it, as long as you stay with the Yankees. Say, there is going to be war, is there not?"

"Yes, there is war already."

"And are you going to be a Yankee soldier?"

"If they will let me. I am rather young, you know."

"Hope you will get killed!" And with this kind wish she left him.

Lawrence was not much surprised when he received a kind letter from his uncle, in which he heartily thanked him for the aid rendered Edward. "Both your aunt and I send you love," he wrote.

Lawrence highly treasured this letter.

CHAPTER XVII

CAMP JACKSON

THE days which followed the firing on Fort Sumter, and the discovery of the programme of Governor Jackson and General Frost, were days of excitement. Although hampered by the officials at Washington who refused to remove Major Hagner, Blair and Lyon bent all their energies to meet the coming storm.

After Governor Jackson had refused, in the most insulting manner, the regiments which President Lincoln had called for from the State, Frank Blair, at once, proffered his regiments of Home Guards which he had raised. They were accepted and Lawrence found himself sworn into the United States service, as Second Lieutenant, to serve in the State of Missouri. He was at once detailed on the staff of Captain Lyon, and placed at the head of his secret service. This was a very responsible position for a boy not yet seventeen years of age. But as we have stated, Lawrence was large for his age, and looked at least two years older than he was. From the time of his appointment up to the day of Lyon's death, Lawrence held the most confidential relations with the General, and learned to love him with his whole heart.

On April 20, the United States arsenal at Liberty, Missouri, was seized, and this in the face of the continued assertions of Governor Jackson and General Frost that they had no designs on United States property in the State. The arsenal was a small one, and contained only four cannon, and about eight hundred muskets. The arms were taken possession of by Frost's State Guards. No apology was offered by Governor Jackson for the seizure.

This action aroused the authorities at Washington. They began to open their eyes to the state of affairs in Missouri. Major Hagner was removed, Lyon made a Brigadier-general of Volunteers, and placed in command of all the troops in St. Louis, and also in control of the arsenal. General Harney was still in command of the Department of the West, but he was soon ordered to Washington to give an account of his stewardship, and this left General Lyon in full command.

Lyon now moved swiftly. He armed five regiments of Blair's Home Guards, kept five thousand more muskets for regiments to be raised in the future and turned over ten thousand muskets to Governor Yates of Illinois with which to arm the Illinois troops then being raised. But Lyon was taking no chances on the remaining arms and munitions of war in the arsenal. On the night of April 26, the steamer *City of Alton* quietly drifted down the river in front of the arsenal, and all the arms which remained were quietly but quickly transferred on board, and by morning were safely in Alton, Illinois.

When St. Louis awoke in the morning, they found nothing in the arsenal worth fighting for. All the plotting of Governor Jackson and General Frost had come to naught. This move on the part of Lyon brought consternation to the hearts of the secessionists. But though they had lost the arms, the city and the State remained to be fought for. The only hope of carrying the State into rebellion was through the organization of the State Guards; and so Governor Jackson and General Frost went on to carry out their programme as planned. It had been the intention of Frost to encamp his State Guards on the hills which commanded the arsenal, so that when the cannon asked for arrived from the South, he could batter down its walls; but the removal of the arms had made this unnecessary. Lyon also had taken the precaution to occupy the hills with his troops; so General Frost established his camp in a beautiful wooded valley, known as Lindell Grove, near the intersection of Olive Street and Grand Avenue. In honor of the Governor, Frost named it Camp Jackson. It was a place that in a few days was to become historic.

In the meantime, Governor Jackson had received a loving letter from President Davis, promising to send the cannon asked for (stolen from the United States arsenal at Baton Rouge), and stating that he was anxiously looking forward to the day when Missouri would take her place in the Confederacy.

On May 6, General Frost was ready to move out to Camp Jackson with his Guards. It was a gala day in St. Louis. Every secessionist in the city was out to see them go. The streets were crowded with an excited, cheering throng. It was a brave man who would have expressed publicly Union sentiments that day. There were about eight hundred of the Guards, the flower of the Southern chivalry of the city. A grand appearance they made, with gay uniforms, prancing horses, and waving flags. Proudly they marched through the streets of the city, cheered by the thousands who thronged the line of march. Fair women waved their handkerchiefs and shouted until their pretty throats were sore. They scattered flowers in the pathway of their heroes, and prophesied that they would sweep from the earth Blair's Dutchmen.

"Any one of those men is a match for ten of Blair's Dutch," was the cry, and that deluded, excited throng believed it.

As for the Union men, and Germans of the city, they had been cautioned to make no demonstration, and to keep away from the line of march; therefore the secessionists had it all their own way. It was a continual ovation from the time Frost started until he reached camp.

Above the camp floated the Stars and Stripes.

Not one of the Guards but loathed that flag and looked upon it with contempt. The excitable women who thronged the camp looked upon it in horror, and demanded that it be lowered.

"You ladies must not be impatient," said an officer. "We have to keep it flying to show that we are true and loyal citizens of the United States, until the time comes for us to change, then, presto, down it comes, and the flag of the glorious Southern Confederacy goes up in its stead."

"I hate hypocrisy," exclaimed a pretty young lady, stamping her foot. "It looks like cowardice, and then you fool no one. Not a person in St. Louis but knows what this camp is for."

"That flag is to protect us from Lyon," replied the officer. "If we flew the Confederate flag, he would be down on us in no time. It is to maintain a semblance of a lawful gathering that we fly it. I hate to see it as badly as you do, and welcome the day we can lower the hateful rag, and trample it beneath our feet."

"How I should like to trample it now," exclaimed the lady, with flashing eyes. "May I, when you lower it?"

"Yes, if you are here," replied the officer, laughing. "Our cause cannot fail, when we have such supporters as you."

For four days, Camp Jackson was a Mecca for every fair rebel in St. Louis. They thronged its streets and avenues. Especially were they desirous of treading on Davis, Lee, and Beauregard Avenues.

In the camp, gay in their trappings, were Edward Middleton, Randolph Hamilton, and Benton Shelley. Their tents were always surrounded by a bevy of the fairest of the fair, for all these were very popular young men, their families the richest and oldest in St. Louis.

"What would you do if Lyon should attack you?" asked one of the ladies of Benton Shelley.

"Do?" he exclaimed, swelling out his breast. "Why, we can wipe out of existence without half trying all the Dutch that Blair and Lyon can bring against us."

"But they say Lyon has five or six thousand men well armed, and you are not a thousand."

"The more the merrier," laughed Benton. "I feel myself equal to ten of the Dutch. My only fear is, Lyon will not attack us."

"Oh! how I should like to see a battle!" exclaimed a romantic young miss, clasping her hands. "It must be just grand."

"My dear young lady," said a gray-haired gentleman standing by, "if you should see one battle, you would never want to see another. I know, for I served through the Mexican War. I fear and tremble when I think of what is coming. These young gentlemen here will prove heroes, but think of the cost, the young and gallant lives blotted out.

But pardon me for interrupting your pleasant talk," and gracefully lifting his hat he walked away.

"He is an old croaker," said Benton scornfully.

"He is nothing of the kind," replied Randolph Hamilton. "I know him well. He was a most gallant officer during the Mexican War. If this war continues, I look to see him a general. But he speaks the truth as to the horror of a battlefield. But for one, I have counted the cost. If our beloved Southland demands that I give my life that she may be free, I am ready."

"Bosh!" replied Benton, "I don't think of dying; it is the glory of war I am after. Let Frank Blair bring on his Dutch minions as soon as he pleases."

And thus the talk went on, while over them waved the despised flag of their country.

General Lyon kept a careful watch of every movement of Frost. Not only that, but Lawrence kept him well informed as to Frost's most secret plans, thanks to Guilford Craig. On May 8, Lawrence received a communication from Craig saying that the long-looked-for cannon from the South had arrived the night before, on the steamer *J. C. Swain.* The cannon were shipped in huge boxes labelled "Marble," and the ammunition in barrels, and all were consigned to Greely & Gale, a well-known Union firm of St. Louis. But the steamer was stopped before it reached the levee, and these goods were taken off.

Lyon now determined to strike; but to be sure there was no mistake, he visited Camp Jackson that he might see for himself. Disguised as a woman, he rode through the camp and found everything just as Guilford Craig had described it in his communication. He came back, and notified Blair that he would capture the camp the next day.

He had a good reason for his haste, having received news from Washington that General Harney had succeeded in getting himself reinstated, and was now on his way back to assume command. With Harney back, Lyon well knew he would not be permitted to capture the camp.

Frost as well as Lyon had his spies, and they reported what Lyon was about to do. Whereupon Frost wrote a most remarkable letter to Lyon, a letter, considering the circumstances, that an honorable man might well hesitate to write, even in war times. In this letter he protested against the seizure of his camp, declaring himself to be a good and law-abiding citizen of the United States. " So far," said he, "as regards any hostility being intended toward the United States or its property or representatives by any portion of my command, and as far as I can learn (and I think I am fully informed), of any other part of the State forces, I can positively say that the idea has never been entertained."

And this when he had just received cannon from Jeff Davis to batter down the walls of the arsenal.

It was a case of as direct lying as any gentleman indulged in during the war. But both General Frost and Governor Jackson were insane with the idea of forcing Missouri out of the Union, and there was no depth of deception to which they would not go to achieve this end. It was just such deception as this that Blair and Lyon had to overcome from the beginning.

Lyon refused to receive this letter, and went on with his preparations to capture the camp. The news spread through the city like wildfire that Lyon was to storm Camp Jackson, and crowds began to throng the line of march, or hasten to the camp. Of course there would be a fight. Frost would not surrender without a fight, and few stopped to consider what a dangerous place a battlefield is.

" What, suh!" exclaimed a gray-haired Southern gentleman, pulling his mustache, "Blair's Dutch minions fight our boys? The boys will eat them up, eat them up, suh."

As Lyon marshalled his forces, the crowd at first looked on in wonder, and then anger broke forth. How dare those Dutch minions attack the chivalry of the city? No cheers for those soldiers as they marched, no waving of handkerchiefs by fair ladies, no flowers strewn in their line of march; but instead, fierce looks of anger, groans and hisses, and vile epithets greeted them from every side.

There goes Blair's First Regiment. Few Germans there, mostly Americans and Irishmen. How bravely they march! Later the regiment was to cover itself with glory at Wilson Creek, leaving nearly half of its number killed and wounded on Bloody Hill.

Here come the German regiments. No holiday soldiers they. Many of them had been in the revolution of 1848, and had fled to this country. Now they were to fight for that liberty they found here, and which they so dearly prized. Straight ahead they march, looking neither to the right nor the left, and the jeers and taunts and foul names hurled at them fall on deaf ears.

Here comes Totten's regular battery, horses prancing, every grim gunner sitting by his piece. May God pity the youths in Camp Jackson if that battery should ever open on them!

And thus they marched, between living walls of cursing, surging, excited men, women, and children, who every instant threatened to burst forth in open riot. If there was Union sentiment in St. Louis, it was dead that day. Cheers for Jeff Davis, and for the Southern Confederacy, were heard on every side.

Being on Lyon's staff, Lawrence frequently had to ride from one end of the column to the other, carrying orders. This brought him into notice, and made him the subject of violent abuse. Many in the crowd knew him. "There goes the renegade," they shouted; "down with the bastard Yankee."

Once Lawrence rode past his uncle's. Both he and his aunt stood on the steps watching the marching soldiers. If they saw Lawrence, they made no sign, but he saw that their faces were pale. "They are thinking of Edward," he thought.

But his uncle had seen him. A gentleman who stood by his side asked, "Who is that young lieutenant who rides so well? He looks every inch a soldier."

"That," answered Mr. Middleton, "is my nephew. A son with Frost, a nephew with Lyon. I begin to realize the horrors of this strife."

"You are not the only family divided in St. Louis!" replied the gentleman. "You are fortunate in having only a nephew on the wrong side. But I do not like the way those Dutch fellows march. They march like trained soldiers, not a mere mob, as we thought they were. Our boys may have some trouble in beating them."

"Frost will not beat them," replied Mr. Middleton, gloomily; "his command is doomed. I only hope he will surrender without a fight."

"What! surrender without firing a gun? That would be a disgrace. The women of the city would rise in wrath, and denounce Frost and his entire command as arrant cowards."

"It is surrender or annihilation," replied Mr. Middleton. "Look at the thousands who are marching against Frost's few hundred. Look at Totten's battery. In five minutes it could sweep the camp out of existence."

"It would be glorious if the boys should fight, if need be, until the last man fell. It would be a Thermopylæ — an Alamo — that would fire the hearts of the South, aye, of the entire nation," answered the gentleman enthusiastically.

"You would not talk like that, if you had a son in the camp," said Mr. Middleton tartly. "I want my son to do his duty, as I know he will, but that he should stand and be shot down, simply for the purpose of firing the Southern heart, I am not willing."

"Ah! excuse me," replied the gentleman, "I can realize the feelings of a father."

Frost stood helpless, as he saw Lyon encircle his camp with lines of steel. He saw Totten's battery planted where it would sweep his camp from end to end. To resist would be suicidal madness. Yet there were hundreds in that camp who would have resisted to the death, if Frost had given the command. Many afterwards gave their lives for their beloved South.

Around the camp, the crowd grew to an immense size. They came to see the Dutch annihilated. Not for a moment did they think but that Frost would fight; and when the surrender came, a howl of rage arose, that sounded like the cry of wild beasts.

The prisoners stacked their arms, and as they did so, Lawrence saw the tears streaming down more than one manly cheek. Oh! it was so galling, so bitter to their pride, that after all their boasting they had to surrender to the despised Dutch. There were some who would have preferred to fight until they died. Others looked relieved and seemed glad that it was all over. As Lawrence rode along the line he saw many that he knew, many who had been his friends. On the face of Randolph Hamilton there was a look of sadness, but also of grim determination. "You gave us no chance this time," he said to Lawrence, "but wait until we can meet you in a fair field!" His cousin Edward saw him, and turned his back without speaking; but Lawrence saw there were tears in his eyes. Benton Shelley saw him, and with a curse he broke his sword across his knee, and dashing down the pieces, exclaimed: "There, take it that way! The next time we meet, I trust it will be on a battle field, where some coward will not surrender us. I have not forgotten that blow; you and I will meet yet."

They met on the battlefield of Wilson Creek.

After yielding up their arms, the prisoners were marched in between two lines of soldiers, preparatory to being taken to the city. The sight inflamed the mob to desperation. Howls of rage and reviling filled the air. Women were there in that excited throng, and they seemed turned into maniacs. Lawrence saw one rush up to a guard, and spit in his face. The guard pushed her back with the butt of his musket, and with his handkerchief coolly wiped his face.

More threatening grew the mob. They surged around the soldiers like the billows of a storm-swept sea. Their cries of rage were like the howling of wolves, as they close in on their prey. Suddenly volleys of stones and any missile which the mob could lay hold of began to fly. Many of the soldiers were painfully hurt, but the stern command came from the officers, "Don't fire."

Thicker and faster fell the stones, then a pistol shot rang out, and another. The soldiers threw up their guns.

"For God's sake, don't fire," shouted Lawrence; "innocent persons will be killed."

For answer, a burly ruffian whipped out a revolver and fired three shots at him in rapid succession. For the fourth shot the fellow drew up his left arm, and was taking deliberate aim, when a soldier sprang forward, and thrust him through with his bayonet.

Now there came a succession of shots. A soldier out of Company F, Third Missouri, fell dead, three or four out of the company fell wounded. Captain

The mob broke in the wildest confusion

Blandorvski, who commanded the company, fell shouting, " Fire! "

The rifles blazed. Other companies took up the command. For a moment the mob stood and fired back, and then broke in the wildest confusion. Shrinking with fear and rage, they fled, trampling down everything before them. Many of the spectators saved themselves by throwing themselves on the ground when the firing commenced. When the smoke lifted from the field, twenty bodies lay still in death, and — the pity of it — two women and one little child in its mother's arms. The capture of Camp Jackson was not bloodless.

After the excitement of the conflict had somewhat subsided, the prisoners were marched down to the arsenal. Again the way was thronged with a cursing, howling mob. Now and then a stone was thrown, but fear kept the mob from using firearms.

A stone struck Lawrence on the head. For a moment he was dazed, but his hat had saved him from severe injury. A soldier threw up his gun to shoot the ruffian who threw it.

" Don't shoot! " shouted Lawrence, " there has been enough bloodshed."

The soldier, with a protest, lowered his gun, and the man slunk back in the crowd, and disappeared. The prisoners were, at length, safely housed in the arsenal, but the excitement throughout the city grew in intensity.

CHAPTER XVIII

THE PANIC

ST. LOUIS never saw a wilder night than the one following the capture of Camp Jackson.

The Confederates were insane with rage. They cursed Frost for not fighting; he should have fought until every man fell. He should have shown a bold front, and the Dutch would have run.

The wildest rumors began to fill the city. Hundreds had been killed. The Dutch had fired wantonly and without provocation on innocent citizens. They had poured volley after volley into the fleeing crowd, killing men, women, and children alike.

Mobs began to fill the streets vowing vengeance. Cries of "Death to the Dutch!" "Death to Lyon!" "Death to Frank Blair!" "Death to every Union Leader!" arose on all sides. Mobs hungry for blood started for the residences of the Union leaders to kill, burn, maim. They were met by policemen, and details of soldiers, and driven back. The house of every prominent Union man had to be heavily guarded. A huge mob attacked the office of the *Democrat,* the Union paper of the city, and it was saved only by the energetic action of the police. The chief of police was an active secessionist, and most of the policemen were sympathizers with the

South, but they did valiant work that night to save the city from mob rule.

All night long the mob raged through the streets. To Lawrence it was a night full of danger, and one he always remembered. He had to take orders here and there; to guide details of troops to points of danger. Much of the time he was alone. During the night he was shot at three different times. More than once he had to clear the way with his trusty sword, the sword given him by his uncle. Half a dozen times he rode men down who tried to stop him.

There was no sleep in St. Louis that night. Those who took no part in the mob sat in their homes, behind bolted and barred doors and windows, fearing the worst. Woe to the German who was caught alone by that mob! In the morning nearly twenty bodies were found in different parts of the city, beaten out of all semblance of humanity.

Morning came, but the rioting did not stop. Mobs still thronged the streets, crying for vengeance on the Dutch. In the afternoon, a regiment was fired into, and two soldiers were killed. The fire was returned, and the mob fled, leaving some twenty of their number dead and wounded on the field.

Outrages on the Germans continued, and they became greatly excited. Threats of retaliation began to be made. These threats became louder and more frequent. Lyon took measures to see that the troops were kept in strict subordination. Officers were to see that not a shot was fired, except in self-defence. The rumor that the Germans were to take a terrible revenge grew. Never did a city change quicker. The bloodthirsty mob became a pack of shivering cowards. "The Dutch are going to sack the city," was the cry. "They are going to murder men, women, and children; they will spare none."

A terrible panic took possession of the city. Thousands upon thousands fled from their homes, in the wildest fear. The levee became packed with people, crowding, fighting to get on board of the steamboats. Hundreds crossed by ferry over into Illinois. The rich battled with the poor for a place on the boats. One insane thought possessed all — to get away before the Dutch commenced their terrible work. Some would snatch a few valuables and flee, leaving all else behind. Others would pack trunks, and offer fabulous sums to have them conveyed to the levee. It was as if a great fire were sweeping over the city, and the inhabitants had to flee or perish.

Lawrence saw this wild stampede, this senseless panic, with amazement. Was this the same city through which mobs surged but yesterday, thirsting for blood? He knew that, even if some of the more violent Germans wished to retaliate, the officers would prevent any excesses. The soldiers were under control; they would do as they were commanded.

With the same iron will with which he moved on Camp Jackson, Lyon would put down any insurrection.

What were those doing whom Lawrence loved, who had been his friends in days past? Had the senseless panic seized them also? He would see. The streets were filled with vehicles of every description, all headed for the levee. Frantic men were rushing around offering large sums for any sort of conveyance which would take their families to the levee. Even on horseback, Lawrence found it no easy task to thread his way through the maze. In places wagons and carriages were locked together, drivers cursing and swearing. On the steps of a palatial mansion, he noticed the owner standing, gesticulating wildly, and shouting at the top of his voice: "Fifty dollars for a conveyance to take my family to the levee. Fifty dollars."

Lawrence knew the gentleman slightly. He reined in his horse, and said: "Mr. Reaves, there is no occasion to get excited. Remain at home; no one will harm you or your family."

Mr. Reaves turned on him in fury. "I know you," he exclaimed. "You have gone with that monster Lyon. You want us to remain here to be massacred."

"You are not in a particle of danger," replied Lawrence.

"Danger!" shouted Mr. Reaves. "Do you not know the Dutch are already at their hellish work, plundering, burning, murdering, ravishing?" and raising his voice he shouted: "A hundred dollars for a conveyance."

An expressman heard the offer; he was going to a place for fifty. He would let that go, and take the hundred. A bargain was struck, and Lawrence rode away disgusted, leaving Mr. Reaves piling his family and a few valuables into the wagon.

Lawrence paid no more attention to what was going on around him, but rode straight for his uncle's. He arrived none too soon. He found the family all ready to take flight. The carriage stood at the door, and the servants were hastily placing in it various articles. The coachman sat in his seat, but Lawrence saw he was shaking with fear. His uncle, usually so cool and collected, was visibly excited, and was giving his orders in a sharp falsetto voice. Edward, who had just been paroled, stood by his father's side, but when he saw Lawrence a scowl came over his face, and without speaking, he turned and went into the house.

"Uncle Alfred! Uncle Alfred!" shouted Lawrence, as he rode up, "What are you doing? There is no danger. Don't subject Aunt Clara to this maddening crush."

"No danger?" asked his uncle, stiffening. "How do you know? All reports say differently. The Dutch have been given their own way. The city is in their power, to do as they please; and we know what that means."

"It is false, entirely false," cried Lawrence. "Do I not know? Am I not on Lyon's staff. Do I not know that rather than see this city sacked, Lyon would turn his regulars against Blair's regiments? How long do you think they would stand before Totten's battery? But there will be no need. While the Germans are greatly excited, the great majority are law-abiding. The German regiments are under perfect discipline. They will obey their officers. Do you think that Blair, Broadhead, Glover, Howe, Filly, and scores of other stanch Union men of the city, would permit the thing that you fear?"

"But they say the German regiments are beyond control, that they have become raging mobs, lost to all discipline," persisted his uncle.

"I tell you it's false, a dangerous, malicious falsehood!" exclaimed Lawrence. "If you stay I will stake my own life on your safety."

Now for the first time, his aunt spoke. "Alfred," she said, "I believe Lawrence is right. You know I never was much in favor of going. This running away savors too much of cowardice. It is not what true Southerners should do. I believe Edward is of my opinion, but he will say nothing, being so cast down over the surrender of Camp Jackson. If he had been in Frost's place, there would have been no surrender. The Guards would have died right there for the South. No, Alfred, I will not go. Order the carriage back."

Lawrence dismounted, and grasping his aunt's hand, said, "Aunt Clara, I am proud of you. I am glad Southern women don't go into the army; if they did there would be no hopes for the Union."

"Thank you Lawrence," replied his aunt. "I am sorry you cannot see the right, but you will find that it will be as hard to conquer the Southern men as the Southern women. Alfred!" she continued, turning to her husband, "did you not hear me? I will not go."

"Very well, Clara," said Mr. Middleton, "it was for your sake I was going. I hope Lawrence is right. I see now that it would not do for Lyon to allow the city to be sacked. James," to the coachman, "put up the horses, lock the barn, and stay close in-doors."

"Uncle, I will place a guard at the house, if you wish," said Lawrence.

"No, no," cried his aunt, "I could not bear to have any of those horrid Home Guards around. I will trust to what you say."

"You need have no fears, there will be no pillage," said Lawrence, as he mounted and rode away, for he had other friends he wished to persuade not to join in the senseless stampede. He first made for the Hamilton residence. Here he found the scare even worse than it was at his uncle's. Randolph had received his parole, and had just returned as Lawrence rode up. He viewed with surprise the panic which had seized the city. "I do not believe," he said to his father, "there is any real danger. There may be isolated cases of outrage, but nothing more. Lyon seems to have his soldiers well in hand."

"Your mother and Dorothy are wild with fear," replied his father, "we must go on their account. Ah! here comes that young Middleton, in the full uniform of a Yankee officer. I wonder what he is here for."

"I should not wonder if it were to say that this panic is foolish," replied Randolph.

"I see you have not yet gone," said Lawrence, as he dismounted, "I have come to try to dissuade you from going."

Just then Dorothy came rushing out of the house, with a birdcage in her hand. Seeing Lawrence, she dropped the bird, and rushed up to him, crying, "Oh! you will save me, won't you? You used to be my friend."

"Save you from what?" asked Lawrence.

"From the Dutch. Oh! they are murdering everybody; they are going to burn the city. They — they will do worse!"

"Yes, I will save you, Dorothy," replied Lawrence gravely. "Not a hair of your pretty head shall be touched. Get over your foolish fears as soon as possible."

Then turning to Mr. Hamilton, Lawrence said, "This is a foolish, a senseless panic. Stay quietly in your house, and there will not be one particle of danger."

"But those awful stories that we hear! It is reported hundreds of citizens have been shot down," said Mr. Hamilton.

"All lies," replied Lawrence. "About thirty have been killed, all in the mobs that fired on the soldiers."

"But I hear the Home Guards fired volley after volley into the mob from mere wantonness," persisted Mr. Hamilton.

"All lies," replied Lawrence. "Randolph knows all about the firing at Camp Jackson. How was it, Randolph?"

"It did not continue long," replied Randolph, "and to tell the truth, father, the Home Guards can not be blamed for firing. They were being shot down by the mob. A captain fell near me, and it was he who gave the command to fire. I have since heard that the captain died from his wound. If Yankees had fired into us, as that mob into the Home Guards, we would have shot and shot to kill."

"Thank you, Randolph," said Lawrence. "I could not have defended them better. You are not only a brave, but a generous foe."

"We will not go; we shall risk it and stay," said Mr. Hamilton.

"You will not regret it, Mr. Hamilton," exclaimed Lawrence. "Tell the ladies I shall consider them under my especial protection."

Lawrence visited several other places. Some persons he found had already gone; others cursed him for a Yankee, and continued their flight; others heeded, and afterwards thanked Lawrence for his advice.

One of the last places he thought of visiting was that of Joseph Craig, the father of Guilford, and step-father of Benton Shelley. When he reached the place, he found the family already getting into the carriage to take flight. Benton had been released on parole, and was supporting his mother who seemed to be on the verge of fainting. "Are n't you coming?" Lawrence heard Benton call to his father.

"No!" answered Mr. Craig, "Guilford and I will stay here, and take what comes."

"Stay, and be butchered, if you want to," shouted Benton, and he commanded the coachman to drive with all speed to the levee.

"You did the wise thing, Mr. Craig," said Lawrence. "And Guilford, how are you? I see you have n't run either."

"All big fools for being scared," replied Guilford, and coming close to Lawrence, he whispered, "Is n't it fun to see them run, after all their big talk? Say, Lawrence, what do you think about my joining the Yankees? I can't do you any more good here, now that Frost is out of business."

"Better think it over seriously before you do that," replied Lawrence; "but I will see you again. Think I will follow Benton now, and see how he gets along."

Thus saying Lawrence rode to the levee. The scene was indescribable. The levee was packed with vehicles of all kinds. The steamboats were black with people, and hundreds shouting, pushing, crowding to get on. Children were crying, women wringing their hands, men swearing, and over all was the fear that the Home Guards would get them.

Benton Shelley, to get as near the river as possible, had crowded his carriage in between some heavy baggage wagons, and before he could avoid it, the carriage was caught and crushed like an eggshell. Lawrence saw the accident, and springing from his horse, he spoke to a negro staggering along with a heavy trunk.

"Here, you," he said, "drop that trunk, and hold this horse until I come back. Quick now; it 's by command of General Lyon!"

The negro dropped the trunk as if it burned him. "Yes, massa, yes, I hold 'em," he gasped, as he took the bridle.

Lawrence leaped to the rescue; those around had hardly noticed the accident, they were too intent on trying to get away. He extricated Mrs. Craig from the ruined carriage. She did not seem to be injured, but was screaming in hysterics. One of Benton's hands was hurt, and he seemed to be dazed.

Gathering Mrs. Craig in his arms, Lawrence spoke to Benton and said, "Follow me." Then he cried, "Make way for this lady, make way, I command!" Even in that struggling crowd his uniform commanded respect. Making his way through the narrow passageway they made for him, meekly followed by Benton, Lawrence carried Mrs. Craig on board the steamer. "Mrs. Joseph Craig," said Lawrence to an officer who asked who she was.

"Ah! yes," replied the officer. "Carry her right into the cabin.

"Her son will care for her now," replied Lawrence.

"You here, Bent?" exclaimed the officer, who seemed to know him well. "I thought old Lyon had you."

"He paroled us all," growled Benton, as he took his mother, and with the help of the officer carried her into the cabin. Neither did he look at Lawrence nor thank him for what he had done.

When Lawrence got back to his horse, he found a white man cursing the negro, and ordering him to let the horse go, and pick up the trunk he had dropped.

For once the negro refused to obey his master. "Fo' de Lawd! can't do it, massa," he exclaimed.

"Gen'al Lyon heself ordered me to hol' dis horse. He kill me if I let him go."

"What 's that you are telling me?" roared his master. "I will make your back smart for this."

The negro was beginning to tremble, when he caught sight of Lawrence.

"Dar he come now," exclaimed the negro joyfully, "dar comes Gen'al Lyon."

The gentleman stared at Lawrence, who said, "I am sorry I detained your negro, but a lady was in danger, and I went to her rescue. I am not General Lyon as your negro thinks, but I am one of his staff."

"I reckon I know you," said the man, "you are the nephew of Alfred Middleton, the one who went over to the Yankees."

"The same," replied Lawrence, "and I request you not to punish your slave here. He is not to blame for dropping your trunk, I made him. But if I were you, I would have him carry it back home."

"When I want your advice, I will ask for it," snapped the man. "Sambo, pick up that trunk, and be quick about it."

Sambo did as he was commanded, and as he did so, Lawrence slipped a dollar in his hand. After that Lawrence rode back to his quarters with a heavy heart. What he had seen made him sad.

General Harney arrived from Washington in the midst of the panic. He was once more in command. When the people heard that Harney was in command once more, the panic subsided. Surely Harney would not let them all be murdered. The leading secessionists came to him, and begged him to send all the German troops out of the city, over into Illinois. This the general promised to do. But when Frank Blair heard the order he flatly told Harney he could not do it; that the German regiments had enlisted to serve in the State of Missouri, not out of it.

General Harney to justify himself in not keeping his promise, issued a proclamation, in which he stated the German troops were out of his control. The fearful ones took this as meaning that he could not control the German troops, that they had mutinied, and that their officers were powerless.

This started the panic afresh, and the same wild scenes were reënacted. To reassure the people the German regiments were removed to their own part of the city, and the regulars were ordered into the business portion. A few weeks before this, the arrival of forty regular soldiers to help to guard the arsenal had thrown the whole city into hysterics, but now Lyon's regulars, under Captain Saxton, were welcomed with open arms.

The panic gradually subsided, and day by day the refugees came creeping back. But they had to come back, to live under, and be protected by, the flag they had trampled under their feet.

CHAPTER XIX

"THIS MEANS WAR"

ACCORDING to Frost's programme, Governor Jackson was to call a special meeting of the Legislature. This was done, and the Legislature met on the second of May. Most of the members were willing tools in the hands of the Governor, ready to do his bidding. On the afternoon of the tenth of May, the Legislature was debating a bill that virtually made the Governor a dictator. During the debate he hastily entered the hall, and announced that Camp Jackson had been captured. The announcement created the utmost excitement. In fifteen minutes the bill was passed, and signed, and the Legislature adjourned for the night.

But Jefferson City was not to sleep in quiet. At midnight, the citizens were aroused by the violent ringing of every bell in the city. Excited, they rushed into the streets to inquire the cause.

"Frank Blair is coming with his Dutch," was the cry. "He will soon be here to burn and ravage."

Jefferson City was soon in the throes of a panic as great as the one that had seized St. Louis. The Legislature was convened in the dead hours of the night, and bills were passed giving the Governor further dictatorial powers. Detachments of State Guards were rushed to the railroad bridges over the Gasconade and the Osage, to hold them against the passage of trains with Blair's troops. The detachment sent to hold the bridge over the Osage, in their excitement burned it, thus preventing the passage of all trains. At that time Frank Blair was in St. Louis, a hundred and forty miles away, with no more thought of going to Jefferson City than he had of going to the moon. But Jefferson City was in a panic all the same. There was hurrying to and fro. Every man armed himself as best he could with shotgun, rifle, sabre, or ancient sword.

The ammunition which the Governor had been collecting, with which to fight the Yankees when the time came, was buried. All the State funds were secreted; and then the citizens waited in fear and trembling for the coming of Frank Blair and his "Dutch cut-throats." When it became known in Jefferson City that Blair had not left St. Louis, that Harney was once more in command, the excitement gradually subsided, and the Governor once more resumed his plotting to drag the State out of the Union. All his scheming so far had failed, but he was not discouraged; he would try another game. He would hold the State to a strict neutrality, and fight all who durst invade the sacred soil of Missouri, be they Federals, Confederates, or Jayhawkers from Kansas.

The Legislature adjourned on the fifteenth of May. It had done all it could do. It had not only made Governor Jackson a military dictator, but had robbed the children of the State, by turning over two million dollars of school money to the Governor, to be used as a military fund. The Governor was also authorized to sell one million dollars in State bonds which were on hand, and to try to borrow one million dollars more. Thus was the State of Missouri robbed of every cent of its public funds, by men who stood at nothing that they might plunge the State into civil war.

With the means at his command the Governor proceeded to organize his State Guards throughout the entire State. Once his militia was thoroughly organized, the State would be at his mercy; but that would take time, and he must try to hoodwink the Federal Government a little longer. So, through faint-hearted Union men and scheming secessionists, General Harney was induced to meet General Sterling Price, who had been appointed to the supreme command of the State Guards.

General Price and General Harney now entered into a most extraordinary compact, known in history as the Price-Harney Agreement. Under this agreement, General Harney was to move no Federal troops in the State from where they were already. He was to allow no more Federal troops to enter the State. In return, General Price was to maintain the peace of the State.

When General Harney suggested to Price that under the Agreement he should cease organizing the State Guards, Price proudly answered that he was organizing the Guards under the State law, and that he could not think of violating a State law. Everybody knew that his State Guards were Confederate troops in disguise; that when the time came they would be used to force the State out of the Union; yet Harney agreed to this nefarious arrangement. It is almost incredible that General Harney should consent to any such agreement. It was known he deeply sympathized with the South, but he had never wavered in his loyalty to the flag. No doubt he believed that in making such an agreement he might save the State the horrors of a civil strife. Hardly was the ink dry on this agreement, when a Confederate mob took possession of the United States arsenal at Liberty, Clay County, Missouri. This was a small arsenal, and contained only about eight hundred muskets and four cannon. History does not record that Governor Jackson or General Price protested against this outrage. Instead, they used the guns to arm the State Guards. Under the agreement, Harney could not move a soldier or raise a finger to protect any property of the United States.

Frank Blair and General Lyon protested at Washington in the strongest terms against this agreement. "By it," they said, "we are bound hand and foot. Governor Jackson and General Price work their own sweet will." Then the Government became alarmed. For once, the authorities at Washington acted promptly. General Harney was removed, and Lyon left in supreme command.

For the first time, Lyon and Blair were free to act. They went to work to formulate the plan of a campaign which would drive the Confederates from the State.

Lawrence being at the head of the secret service, became an important personage. It was his duty to collect all facts on which Blair and Lyon should act. To do this he began to organize a body of scouts and spies. He had a meeting with Guilford Craig, who again reiterated his determination to enter the Federal service as a scout and spy. There was something in the business, dangerous as it was, which seemed to attract the boy. Naturally secretive, he took delight in deception. That he had deceived General Frost afforded him the keenest satisfaction. But to become a regular scout and spy, his identity would have to be known to the commanding General. To this he consented.

Lawrence, to prepare General Lyon for the meeting, told him who had been his unknown correspondent, and what was now his wish. He also gave the General a full history of Guilford, as far as he knew. The General listened with the closest attention.

"So your spy was an orderly at Frost's headquarters?" said Lyon. "From the information given I knew it must be some one close to Frost. Let me see him, by all means."

When Guilford was introduced to the General, Lyon looked over the slim, rather effeminate-appearing youth, as if he would read him through and through.

"Rather young," was his first remark.

"I am nearly a year older than the Lieutenant, here," said Guilford, pointing at Lawrence.

"You certainly have done good work so far," replied Lyon; "but do you realize what you ask? To be a spy means hardship, cunning, and courage of the highest order. To be captured means an ignominious death. Under the peculiar conditions existing you ran no risk of your life by spying on General Frost, but what you ask now is different."

"I understand fully what it means to be a spy," replied Guilford. "I am not only ready, but eager to become one. I have no fears of death. My life, General, has not been a happy one. Many a time I have been on the point of killing myself. And I am not so frail as I look. Excitement does me good.

I am growing stronger every day. I have never really lived until the last few weeks — that is, outside of my books."

"What books do you read," asked the General sharply.

"Adventures principally. Also novels — Cooper's, Scott's, and Revolutionary tales."

"Ah! I see," said the General. "Unhappy at home, so you have lived an imaginary life of adventure." Turning to Lawrence, he said, "Lieutenant, enroll him as a scout, and let him act under your directions."

Thus Guilford Craig became a regular accredited scout and spy to General Lyon. Only a couple of days after he was appointed, he reported to Lawrence that he wanted to go to Jefferson City. " I want to find out what they are doing there, " he remarked, with a grim smile.

"Do you think the folks at your home have any idea of what you are doing?" asked Lawrence.

" Not in the least. They believe I am a ranting Reb, like Bent. My loving step-mother is trying to get Bent to stay at home, and let me do the fighting for the family. But Bent has the war fever bad, they can't keep him from going; and I reckon he will go shortly. They say the paroles we gave at Camp Jackson are no good. A great many of the boys have already left to join Price. I think I shall have to go."

"What! to join Price?" asked Lawrence.

"Not exactly, but to be around where he is. But I hope Bent will take a notion to go before I do. I believe he intends to do you injury, if he gets a chance. He has never forgiven you for knocking him down. I heard him say only yesterday, that he would almost rather have had his mother hurt in the crush, than to have you help her. Look out for him."

"I will try to look out for myself," replied Lawrence. "He assaulted me once, and got the worst of it."

"Yes, but remember you had a stout German with you. What if you had been alone?" asked Guilford.

"I will be careful; so if you want to go to Jefferson City, don't stay on my account."

The next day Guilford was gone, and Lawrence in his many duties forgot his warning, but it was to be brought to his mind very forcibly. The very next evening, as he was carrying an order to Captain Saxton, he was fired upon from a dark alley, the bullet passing through his hat. Quick as thought he returned the fire, and his would-be assassin fled. The firing hurriedly brought a guard, but whoever had fired the shot made good his escape.

Lawrence had but little doubt as to whom his assailant was. He told his suspicions to General Lyon, and Lyon ordered him to have young Shelley watched by some of his secret men. But in some way Benton found that he was under suspicion, and fled from the city.

The stories which the refugees who flocked to St. Louis told showed that the life of no Union man in Missouri was safe outside of the large cities. Outrages were being committed every day, and this was the "safety" which Jackson and Price promised, for being allowed to have their own way.

On the fifth day after Guilford Craig had left for Jefferson City, Lawrence was surprised at his return.

"I have been having the time of my life," he said with a laugh. "No trouble to get news in Jefferson City, if you work it right. I was undecided whether to go in disguise or as Guilford Craig. I concluded to go as Guilford Craig, as that would disarm suspicion. When it became known that I was the son of Joseph Craig, and that I was one of Frost's men captured at Camp Jackson, I was a hero right away. I was introduced to both Jackson and Price. They asked me many questions, and were somewhat surprised at the information I possessed. But when I told them I was an orderly for General Frost, they ceased to wonder. I also gave them to understand that I was so situated, that I could obtain much valuable information from the Union side. They then questioned me very sharply, and asked me to return the next day, as they might have a proposition to make.

"In the meantime I had fallen in with several of the boys from St. Louis whom I knew, and the way we hurrahed for Jeff Davis, and damned Lincoln was a caution. I think Price had spies watching me, but if so he was satisfied, for the next day when I met Jackson and Price they were very gracious, and when I left them, what do you think I was?"

"I don't know," replied Lawrence. "It is hard to tell what you will do."

"I am a duly accredited spy, in the employ of General Price."

"What!" exclaimed Lawrence in surprise.

"Fact. In what way could I get so much news?"

"But the danger," said Lawrence. "You may be putting your neck in a noose."

Guilford laughed. "That is what makes the game worth the playing," he answered. "If there were no danger, there would be no excitement."

"It's a game I would not care to have a hand in," said Lawrence. "What did you learn at Jefferson City?"

"Nothing startling, yet many things of importance. Jefferson City is full of generals, colonels, and other officers not so important, of the State Guards. The entire efforts of Jackson and Price now are to organize the Guards all over the State as soon as possible. They are playing for time now, and the conservative Union men are the cards they are using. They want to hold Lyon back as long as possible, and so they want to talk compromise until the last moment.

"But here is the programme in full:

"'*First:* Fire the hearts of the people, by claiming that the shooting at Camp Jackson was entirely unprovoked, that it was simply a massacre, as was the firing on the mob the next day.

"'*Second:* Organize the State Guards in every county, officered by men known to be true to the South. In the meantime let the driving out and terrorizing of the Union men continue in full blast.

"'*Third:* Call an election to decide whether Missouri shall secede or not. At this election see that as few Union men vote as possible. Make it all a man's life is worth to vote for the Union. See that the State Guards do their duty, as to preventing Union men voting.

"'*Fourth:* As soon as the State votes for secession, turn the State over to the Confederacy.'"

"It's a lovely plan," said Lawrence. "Let us lose no time laying it before Blair and Lyon."

This was done, Guilford coming in disguise, so he would not be known, if any of his Confederate friends saw him.

Lyon listened to Guilford's report in silence, until he was through, but Lawrence saw a look of surprise come over his face when Guilford told of being employed as a spy by General Price.

"What do you think, Blair?" asked Lyon, after Guilford had made his report.

"His report tallies with what I hear from all over the State," said Blair. "A reign of terror exists, and no Union man is safe. Not only that, but they are getting many people to believe that the taking of Camp Jackson was uncalled for, and that firing on the mob was murder."

"But what of this young man becoming a spy for General Price? It will be hard for him to satisfy both sides."

"That," replied Blair, "is a game which can be played easily now, but not when both armies are in the field. The State Guards are not Confederate troops yet, therefore the Confederate Government could not claim young Craig as a spy, even if captured."

"I think that would not save him, if they knew, but we will talk of this afterwards," answered Lyon; "now we must act on the information received. Some of the plans of Jackson and Price are already giving me trouble. I am being harassed to death by weak-kneed Union men, to meet Jackson and Price, to see if a compromise cannot be arranged. The fools! to think of a compromise now when both North and South are marshalling thousands of men who will soon meet in the shock of battle."

"Better meet them, and have it done with," remarked Blair.

"I believe it will be for the best," answered Lyon. "I will send Jackson and Price a safe conduct tomorrow."

Lyon did so, and Jackson and Price came on to St. Louis to meet Lyon and Blair. This meeting, which is historic, took place at the Planter's House, on the eleventh day of June. On one side were Governor Jackson, General Price, and Thomas L. Snead. On the Union side, General Lyon, Frank Blair, and Major Conant. The meeting lasted four or five hours. Colonel Snead in speaking of it said: "Lyon held his own at every point against Jackson and Price, masters though they were of Missouri politics."

With Jackson and Price it was the same old story of deceit and subterfuge. They would go on organizing the State Guards. The Federal Government must not interfere. No United States soldiers must be brought into the State, none must be enlisted in the State. Those already there must not be moved from where they were.

Disgusted, Lyon abruptly closed the discussion by saying: "Rather than concede to the State of Missouri the right to demand that my Government shall not enlist troops within her limits, or bring troops in whenever she pleases, or move troops at her own will into, out of, or through the State;

rather than concede to the State of Missouri for one single instant the right to dictate to my Government in any matter however unimportant, I would" — rising and pointing to each one in the room in turn — "see you, and you, and you, and you, and every man, woman, and child in the State, dead and buried. *This means war*." Without another word, he turned and left the room, his sword clanking by his side.

For a time there was a death-like silence in that room. Not a man there but was every inch a soldier, but they all paled at Lyon's words. These words meant to Jackson and Price loyalty to the Union, or war. They chose war.

For four years Missouri was to be furrowed with the red-hot plough-share of internecine strife. It was a war more horrible than visited any other State. On the Union side it meant war with the guerilla bands of Quantrel Anderson, and scores of others as bloody. On the Confederate side, it meant Jennison, with his Jayhawkers, the devastation of homes, arrests, prison; it meant cold-blooded murders, men shot down in the presence of their families; it meant a war in which the black flag was raised, and no quarter given. That is what Governor Jackson gave the State he professed to love, when he chose war.

CHAPTER XX

THE ADVANCE ON JEFFERSON CITY

"LIEUTENANT MIDDLETON," said General Lyon, as he entered his headquarters after his memorable interview, "Governor Jackson and General Price are at the Planter's Hotel. See that they leave the city in an hour. If they are in the city at the expiration of that time, arrest them."

Lawrence saluted, and taking an orderly with him, proceeded to the hotel, but found both Jackson and Price ready to take their departure. They had come on an extra train, and lost no time in taking it back to Jefferson City. He rode down to the depot, to see them off. "How I should like to arrest them," thought he, "but they know what is good for them, and will get away in time."

As the train moved out, he was surprised to see Guilford Craig board the rear car. "What will that boy be doing next?" muttered Lawrence. "If he keeps on, he will soon be hobnobbing with Jeff Davis."

He would have known what Guilford was doing, if he had been on the train, for hardly was it out of the station, before he was in close conversation with the Governor and the General. It was a great story he told them. Lyon had fifteen thousand soldiers — they were all ready to march — Lyon would not wait a minute after their safe conduct was out — no doubt he was already making up trains to pursue them, or loading his troops on steamboats.

"How do you get all your information?" asked General Price.

"From a friend who is close to Frank Blair," answered Guilford, without hesitation. "He poses as a great friend of the Union, on purpose to get information."

Both Governor Jackson and General Price were much depressed by what Guilford told them.

"Governor, if what Craig tells us is true, and I have heard the same from others," said the General, "it will be impossible for us to hold Jefferson City. Lyon will be on us in two or three days, and it will be impossible for me to bring over two thousand poorly armed men to oppose him."

The Governor groaned. "It will be a terrible blow to our cause to give up the capital," he exclaimed. "Where will you concentrate, if the capital is given up?"

"At Boonville," was the answer. "But if Lyon moves with celerity, even that will have to go, and then Lexington. I am in hopes I can hold Lexington. If the State Guards answer your call as I think they will, in two weeks I ought to be able to have ten thousand troops at Lexington. Time — time is what I want, but I am afraid Lyon will not give it to me."

"I will spoil his fun in moving on the railroad," said the Governor. "I will order the bridges over the Gasconade and the Osage to be burned as soon as we pass over them. This should delay Lyon at least two days."

Guilford had heard all he wished, so he suggested that they let him off at the first station, and he would go back and watch the movements of Lyon. This pleased both the Governor and the General, so Guilford left the train at the first stop to make his way back to the city.

Both the Governor and General Price were thoroughly alarmed. They reached Jefferson City at two o'clock in the morning, but there was no sleep for them. A proclamation was prepared and telegraphed over the State calling for fifty thousand men to drive the Federal army off the sacred soil of Missouri.

The citizens became intensely excited when it became known that the city was to be given up without a struggle. Curses loud and deep were hurled at the officials. Many of the more prominent secessionists hurriedly packed their goods in wagons, and fled to the country. Others who had been rampant secessionists suddenly became good Union men.

Lyon knew that time meant everything to him,

and he did not lose a moment in making preparations to strike a telling blow before General Price
had time to concentrate any considerable force. Lyon
did not have an available force of over five thousand
men, but he did not hesitate. Dividing this small
force into two divisions he made preparations for
an immediate advance. One division, under Sigel
and Sweeney, was to strike for Southwest Missouri.
The other division, consisting of scarcely two thousand men, he was to lead himself up the Missouri,
and strike the force of General Price, which he
supposed would concentrate at Jefferson City. He
was soon to learn that General Price had concluded
to abandon Jefferson City, and make his first stand
at Boonville; and this news was brought by Guilford Craig.

On the forenoon of the twelfth, an orderly came
to Lawrence and told him a young man who in-
sisted he must see Lieutenant Middleton, had been
stopped by the guard. He said he must see him as
quickly as possible, as he had important information
to impart.

" Bring him to me," said Lawrence.

The orderly soon returned accompanied by a slim,
rather delicate-looking youth with a brown mustache, and rather long, dark, curling hair. Lawrence glanced at him, and did not recollect ever having seen him before.

"You wished to see me, I believe?" questioned

Lawrence. " I have but a moment to spare, as I am very busy. What is it?"

" My information is for your ears alone," replied the youth in a soft Southern accent.

Lawrence made a sign to the orderly, who at once withdrew. No sooner were they alone than the young man by a quick movement removed his false mustache and hair, and Guilford Craig stood before him.

For a moment Lawrence could only stand and stare in astonishment; then he exclaimed, " Guilford, as I live! I should never have known you. But how did you come here? I could swear I saw you board the Governor's train last night."

" So you did, but I rode with them only a few miles. I found out all I wanted, so dropped off and came back. How do you like my disguise?"

" Capital. You completely fooled me; but why do you assume it?"

" Because it would never do for Guilford Craig, who is a red-hot Rebel, and in the employ of General Price, to be seen hobnobbing with General Lyon, or holding a secret conference with Lieutenant Middleton, his chief of secret service. When I am with you I am Charles Morris, at your service. Please remember."

" All right, Morris," replied Lawrence with a smile, " what have you learned?"

" That Governor Jackson and General Price are

scared out of their wits. When I say 'scared,' I don't mean they are physically afraid, for they are both brave men, as brave as men are made, but they are frightened over the situation. The suddenness of Lyon's movement has taken them by surprise, and they are not prepared. I heard General Price say, 'Oh! if he would only give us two weeks!' I told them Lyon had fifteen thousand men, and without doubt would move on Jefferson City without delay. General Price then said it would be impossible to hold the capital, and that he would concentrate his forces at Boonville and Lexington. The Governor hated to give up Jefferson City, but at last consented to the plan of the General. They were afraid General Lyon might move by rail, and therefore the Governor said he would give orders to have the bridges over the Gasconade and the Osage burned as soon as their train had passed over them."

"General Lyon must know this immediately," said Lawrence.

Therefore Guilford was conducted to the General to whom he told his story. Lyon listened attentively and then said, " I have just received word from a trusty agent that the bridges are burning, but it makes little difference, for I shall move by boat; yet it might be well to make a diversion by rail, as far as the Gasconade. The earliest I can get away by boat is to-morrow."

Lawrence jumped at the idea of a diversion by rail. "General," he exclaimed, "why not make a diversion by rail this afternoon. We can make a great show of force. The train can come back during the night. As for me, I ask the privilege of taking a small party to scout through to Jefferson City on the south side of the river. If Price is to evacuate the city, there will be no force of State troops of any size on this side."

The General thought a moment, and then asked how large a party he would need for the scout.

"Not more than four or five men besides myself," answered Lawrence. "A large party would defeat my object, that of gaining information."

"But they would know you were Federals by your uniforms," said the General.

"That is the reason I desire a small party," said Lawrence, "we would go as citizens, not as soldiers."

"It would be somewhat dangerous," replied the General. "I would not order you to take such a risk, but if you desire to take the scout, I will not order otherwise."

Lawrence was overjoyed at the permission. Orders were at once given to prepare an extra train. It was to consist of several cars, with about two hundred soldiers. These were to make a show as if the cars were crowded. Lawrence chose Guilford, Carl Mayer, and two more good and true men to accompany him on the scout. They took five horses without brands, in a box car. For arms they took two revolvers each.

By two o'clock all was ready, and the train started. They found great crowds at every station through which they passed, and the country intensely excited.

"The Yankees have come!" "The Yankees have come!" was the cry. The train was greeted with curses, mingled with cheers. At Herman, the last town before they reached the Gasconade, there was an immense crowd. They knew the bridge over the river had been burned, and the soldiers were greeted with, "You have gone about as far as you will. Pop Price is too smart for you. You don't get to Jefferson City to-day, and when you do get there you will find a warm reception."

Finding the crowd turbulent, and disposed to mischief, half of the force was left there, and the word was given out that if any person was found tampering with the railroad track he would be shot at once. Before the guns and bright bayonets of the soldiers, the crowd sullenly dispersed. With the rest of the soldiers, the train cautiously proceeded on its way to the Gasconade. The bridge was still burning, and some horsemen were watching it from the opposite side. A few shots were fired, and the horsemen fled precipitately, and word was telegraphed to Jefferson City that the Yankee

army was already as far as the Gasconade. This
news hastened the flight of the Governor and General Price from the capital.

The train was backed up and stopped in a wood,
where it was concealed from observation. Here
Lawrence and his little party left the train. They
had come prepared, and all were dressed in citizens'
clothes. It was now dark, and with many hand-
shakes and wishes for success, the officers on the
train bade them good-bye.

Said the Major in command: "Boys, I had
rather go back than be in your boots. You will be
lucky if you are not all swinging at the ends of
ropes in less than two days."

"A cheerful prospect surely," replied Lawrence,
"but I trust you will prove a false prophet."

"Well, take care of yourself, and keep your pow-
der dry," remarked the Major, as he stepped on
board the now moving train, and Lawrence and his
companions were left alone — alone in the midst of
enemies.

They held a consultation, and resolved to pass
themselves as young men from St. Louis on their
way to join Price's army. They also concluded to
ride some miles south before crossing the Gasconade.
This would also take them away from the railroad,
and thus they should avoid the towns. Finding a
road which led south, they rode at a good pace
for some half an hour, when they began to think of

trying to secure lodgings for the night. Meeting a man, they asked if he knew of any place that would be apt to keep them. He scratched his head, and then slowly replied:

"I reckon Cunnel Bell would, if you'n be of the right sort. He lives about a mile farther on."

"What do you call the right sort?" asked Lawrence.

"Well, the Cunnel is a tearing secessionist. Form your own conclusions."

"I see," replied Lawrence, laughing. "Many Southern men around here?"

"Yes, there is right smart."

"Any Union men?"

"A sprinklin', but they keep mighty quiet."

"Which side do you train with?" asked Lawrence.

"Look here, stranger, air you'ns tryin' to get me into trouble?" asked the man, evidently very uneasy. "I am a peaceable citizen, I am. I told you'ns the Cunnel was a tearing Southern man. Is n't that enough?"

"Quite enough," said Lawrence, "and we thank you for the information. Good-night," and they rode on.

The man shook his head, as he watched them disappear. "Now, I wonder who they be," he asked himself. "If they be Union, thar will be trouble if they stop at the Cunnel's. If they be secesh, the Cunnel will give them the best he has. Wanted to know which side I trained with! If Silas Kemp knows himself, he is keeping mighty mum nowadays."

It proved a long mile to Colonel Bell's. As the night was quite dark, they could see but little of the place, but the house proved a large and imposing one. In answer to their hail, a negro came to the door, and asked, "Who is dar?"

"Tell your master," said Lawrence, "that five young men from St. Louis, and on their way to Price's army, have been belated, and crave entertainment for the night."

The negro disappeared, and in a moment a white-haired gentleman with a decided limp came to the door.

"If you are what you represent," said the Colonel, "you are more than welcome. Please dismount. Jim," turning to the negro, "call Rufus and Tom, and see that the gentlemen's horses are cared for."

The Colonel then ushered his guests into the house. Everything showed that it was the abode of wealth and refinement. The Colonel first asked if they had had supper, and on being answered in the negative, he gave orders that a meal be prepared.

"May I ask," said the Colonel, "whom I entertain? And as you are from St. Louis, I trust you can give me all the news."

Before Lawrence could answer, Guilford spoke

up. "Allow me, Colonel Bell, to introduce to you, our leader, Lieutenant Middleton, the son of Alfred Middleton, the well known banker of St. Louis. This gentleman," pointing to Carl Mayer, " is Randolph Hamilton, and I am Benton Shelley, the stepson of Joseph Craig. These other two gentlemen are named Harris and Sherman, both sons of prominent citizens of St. Louis."

During this remarkable recital, Lawrence and the others could only sit and stare in astonishment at the temerity of Guilford. They durst not contradict him, so remained silent. But the effect on their host was apparent.

" Gentlemen, I had no idea," he exclaimed, " I was so highly honored by your presence. Although every friend of the South is welcome here, you are doubly so. I am personally acquainted with your father, sir," bowing to Lawrence, "and Messrs. Hamilton and Craig I know by reputation. But if I may ask, what fortune or misfortune has brought you here?"

Lawrence, seeing the deception must now be kept up, said, "Three of us were with Frost's command when taken prisoners at Camp Jackson. Our paroles have since been declared illegal, and we are at liberty to fight for the cause we so love. But Frank Blair and General Lyon have St. Louis by the throat. To enlist in the State Guards, we have to steal out of the city. This we did, but when we reached Herman we were surprised by a train-load of Yankee soldiers."

"What? Yankee soldiers at Herman?" asked the Colonel in surprise.

"Yes. Have you not heard the latest news?" asked Lawrence.

"No, I was in Jefferson City Sunday, and was so unfortunate as to severely strain my ankle in stepping from the train. Governor Jackson and General Price were then trying to arrange a meeting with Lyon to see if some sort of a compromise could not be effected. They are fighting for time. If they can only get the State Guards thoroughly organized, they can drive the Yankees from the State."

"The meeting took place yesterday," said Lawrence. "Lyon would yield nothing, and gave the Governor and General Price an hour in which to leave the city. They came back to Jefferson City last night, and gave orders for the railroad bridges over the Gasconade and Osage to be burned. If this had not been done, the Yankees we saw at Herman would be in Jefferson City by this time."

"But Price will hold Jefferson City against the Yankee cut-throats," exclaimed the Colonel.

"There is a rumor that he has already given orders for its evacuation," replied Lawrence.

The Colonel leaped from his chair in his excitement, forgetting his lame ankle. "Impossible! Impossible!" he cried. "General Price and the State

Lawrence saw the General reel in his saddle

[*Page 324*]

Guards will die right there before they will yield up Jefferson City."

"The rumor may be false; we can only hope for the best," replied Lawrence, giving his answer a Delphic meaning.

Here supper was announced, and the boys were introduced to the Colonel's wife and daughter, the latter a lovely girl of twenty who was all graciousness, and who was positive the Yankees could never capture Jefferson City. The next morning a royal breakfast was given them, and the party were sent on their way, amid the best wishes of the whole household. The young lady extracted a promise from Lawrence that he would surely call if ever he came that way again.

"The Lieutenant has made a conquest," chuckled Guilford, as they rode away. "She is a beauty, all right; would n't mind if I were in the Lieutenant's boots."

"Guilford, how could you deceive those good people so?" asked Lawrence. "It was bad enough for us to represent that we were going to join Price's army. What would my cousin think, if he knew I had been masquerading under his name?"

Guilford threw back his head, and gave one of the heartiest laughs Lawrence ever heard him give. "That was just rich," he exclaimed; "I wish the boys might know some day."

They knew sooner than Guilford thought, for

Lawrence and his party had been gone hardly an hour when three horsemen rode up to Colonel Bell's to inquire the best way to get across the Gasconade, saying they were from St. Louis, and on their way to join Price.

"I am glad to see so many of you young men from St. Louis on your way to join General Price," said the Colonel. "Five young men, all fine fellows and from the best families of St. Louis, stayed with me last night, on their way to join Price."

"Do you know who they were?" queried one of the three, much interested.

"Yes. One was the son of the rich banker, Alfred Middleton, another was Randolph Hamilton, the son of Judge Hamilton, and a third was Benton Shelley, who said he was the step-son of Joseph Craig, the rich broker. I believe the names of the other two were Harris and Sherman."

The three young men looked at each other in utter astonishment. For a moment surprise rendered them speechless; then one exclaimed, "You have been most grossly deceived. I am Edward Middleton, the son of Alfred Middleton; this gentlemen," pointing to one of his companions, "is Randolph Hamilton; and this one," pointing to the remaining one, "is Benton Shelley. There has been queer work here for some reason."

"You may depend that precious cousin of yours is at the bottom of this," spoke up Benton Shelley.

"Describe them," they all demanded at once.

Colonel Bell did the best he could, but the only one recognized was Lawrence.

"Yes, no doubt my cousin was at the bottom of the whole thing," said Edward, bitterly. "The reason is plain. He is at the head of the Secret Service of General Lyon. He is spying out the land. It is easy for him with a small party, to ride through the country, taking our names and representing that they are on the way to join Price."

"The whole party will swing if we can catch them," eagerly exclaimed Benton. "How long do you say they have been gone?"

"About an hour," said Colonel Bell.

"Let us after them," cried Benton, "by hard riding I believe we can overtake them."

But this was overruled by Edward and Randolph under the plea that it might injure the horses. But the fact was, Edward did not wish to engage in a conflict with his cousin.

Little thinking that their identity had been discovered, Lawrence and his party continued on their way, congratulating themselves that so far their trip had been a success. Their route led them some miles south of Jefferson City, and along in the afternoon as they turned to ride direct to the city, they were surprised to meet numerous vehicles filled with household goods, and carriages loaded down with women and children. From all whom they met came the same story: The city was in a terrible state of excitement, and was being deserted by the State troops. The Governor and General Price were preparing to flee. The Yankees were expected any moment, and would not be opposed. The city would be at their mercy, and there was no knowing what would happen when they took possession.

Lawrence and his party were urged not to enter the city, but to keep on west to Tipton, where General Parsons was retreating with the State troops which had fled from the capital. But Lawrence said that he would investigate the situation before joining Price.

When they neared the city, a halt was made, and Carl Mayer said: "There are a great many Germans in Jefferson City, and though they have had to keep quiet, I know they are as true to the Union as are the Germans of St. Louis. I am personally acquainted with several Germans who live here. Let me go ahead and investigate."

This was agreed to, and the little party withdrew to a wood where they were screened from observation, and Carl rode on alone. He was gone so long that it became dark, and Lawrence began to be alarmed over his absence, when he appeared with the good news that he had found an old friend, and that they would be welcomed gladly. "I found the Germans of the city secretly organized," he said, "and we shall be perfectly safe."

Carl led the way, and it was not long before they were under a hospitable German roof, the first of Lyon's army to enter Jefferson City.

CHAPTER XXI

BOONVILLE

CARL'S German friend was named Kuenster, and judging from the meal which Mrs. Kuenster set out for our hungry scouts, famine had not come to Jefferson City, even if it were war time. After their hunger had been fully satisfied, Lawrence and Guilford took a stroll around the little city. They found the streets filled with excited citizens, and the one topic of conversation was the desertion of the city by the State authorities, and the coming of Lyon. The Unionists, who for months had lived in fear and trembling, not daring to avow their sentiments, now began to assert themselves, and cheers were heard for the Union and for Lyon.

As for the Southern element, they were completely dumbfounded by the desertion of their leaders. As we have noticed, many of the more prominent secessionists had left the city, and others were preparing to leave. Those who expected to remain became very quiet, and there were some sudden conversions to the Union side. Lawrence found that the State troops under General Parsons had left during the forenoon, going west. His force was estimated at one thousand. Governor Jackson and General Price with their staffs had taken passage on a steamboat and gone up the river. Governor Jackson was never to enter the capital again. He had waged a desperate fight, and lost. When the little steamboat on which he was, steamed up the river, and the capital faded from view, it was in the book of Fate that he should never see it again.

After learning all he could, Lawrence returned to Mr. Kuenster's, where he resolved to remain quietly until Lyon came.

The next morning Guilford announced his intention of taking a scout by himself. Privately he told Lawrence that his destination was the camp of General Parsons. " I want," he said, "to find out where he has gone, and what his orders are."

Lawrence demurred, on account of the danger, but Guilford only laughed. " This disguise," he said, " will come off, and I shall go as Guilford Craig, and Guilford Craig is a privileged character among the State troops. What do you think of this?" and he handed Lawrence a paper.

Lawrence took it, and to his astonishment read:

To all officers and soldiers of the Missouri State
    Guards:
  Pass the bearer, Guilford Craig, at all times, and
in all places, without question.
  By order of General Sterling Price,
        Com. Missouri State Guards.

"When did you get this?" asked Lawrence.

"That evening on the cars. Why should he not give it to me? Am I not one of his trusted spies?"

"It is a desperate game you are playing, Guilford. Surely you have to give General Price some information of value, or he would mistrust you."

"The information I give him will never lead him to any great victory," said Guilford, smiling. "I am careful. My value is the information that I will give General Lyon. Have no fear of me. I shall be back sometime to-morrow. Good-bye, until I see you."

Lawrence watched him as he rode away, and the thought flashed across his mind, "What if he is deceiving me, and General Lyon, and is in reality a spy for Price?" But he put the thought away as unworthy, after all that Guilford had done. Carl and the other two soldiers with Lawrence were a little curious to know what had become of the man they knew as Charles Morris, but Lawrence told them he was out on a little scout of his own, and that satisfied them.

During the day the same excited crowds thronged the streets, and more than once the cry was raised that Lyon was coming. As Lawrence well knew, these were false alarms, but in the afternoon he had a surprise, and for a time it looked as if he might have more excitement than he wished. He and Carl were idly loitering through the city, but keeping their eyes open, when on turning a corner they suddenly came face to face with the three young gentlemen they had personated at Colonel Bell's. There was no way of escape. It is hard to say which party was the more astonished. For a moment, they could only stare at each other, then almost involuntarily the hands of the three Confederates went to their hip pockets, and Carl's did the same. Lawrence saw the movement. Above all things he wished no street fight, especially with his cousin.

"Don't be a fool, I have more friends here than you think," he said to Edward in a low voice, then exclaimed in a joyful tone, as if he had met a dear friend, "Why, Edward, is that you? Glad to see you. How in the world did you come here?"

"Not as you did, under an assumed name," retorted Edward surlily. "And when you desire to change your name again, please don't dishonor mine by taking it."

Lawrence colored. "You must have stopped at Colonel Bell's after we left," he said. "All is fair, you know, in time of war. But I will try not to transgress again."

"It was a blame sharp trick," exclaimed Randolph. "Who personated me?"

"I had that honor," said Carl.

"What! a German personate a Hamilton? That is a little tough on me, is it not, Carl?"

"Not as tough as it was on me," answered Carl.

All this time Benton Shelley had stood by scowling, not saying a word, his hand still at his hip pocket.

" These fellows are spies," he growled. " Why not give the alarm, have them arrested and hanged as they ought to be?"

" Softly," replied Lawrence, "this city has been evacuated by the State forces. If any are spies you are the ones. It will be good for your health to get out of here before Lyon comes."

By this time they had attracted attention, and a crowd began to gather. A policeman put in an appearance, and ordered the crowd to disperse. The city authorities did not wish to have any riot, and Lyon was expected any moment. Neither did Lawrence wish to have attention attracted to him.

Edward, Randolph, and Benton held a consultation, and a short time afterwards were seen to ride out of the city. After they had left Colonel Bell's, they had heard that Jefferson City had been evacuated by the State forces, and they had decided to ride into the city and spy out the land. But after being discovered by Lawrence, they concluded it would be the part of discretion to depart before Lyon came.

As for Lawrence, he rejoiced that Guilford was not with him. Benton might have seen through his disguise. The rest of the day and night passed quietly. The next day about noon, Guilford Craig came. His horse showed it had been ridden hard. To the question as to where he had been, he replied he had been visiting friends in the country. At the first opportunity Lawrence sought a private interview with him.

"It is all right," he told Lawrence. "General Parsons is a bully fellow, and when I showed him that paper of General Price's, he fell all over himself to tell me all he knew. He has about a thousand men, and has orders to stop at Tipton, and to hold his command in readiness to march to Boonville, if Lyon concludes to move on that place after he occupies Jefferson City. General Price is not at Boonville, he went on to Lexington. Governor Jackson stopped at Boonville. Marmaduke is there with less than a thousand men. If Lyon moves rapidly, he can get there before Parsons possibly can, and capture it as easy as shooting. He ought to be here by this time."

"Guilford, you are a wonder," said Lawrence, "but I tremble when I think of the risk you run."

"Pshaw!" replied Guilford, "it's fun, and just think of the excitement I am having. And then I am out for revenge. I am working to revenge my poor black mammy. I hope this war will never stop until every slave is free. Lawrence, you have no idea of the impression the fate of poor Hannah had upon me. What she suffered she suffered for my sake. I can never forget it."

Lawrence said no more. He saw that as a lonely, loveless child, he had brooded over the fate of the black woman who had nursed and loved him, until it had become a monomania with him.

Just then there was a cry raised that Lyon was coming, and an excited throng began to pour down to the bank of the river. Down the river hung a great cloud of smoke pouring from the stacks of coming steamboats. Nearer and nearer they came, and it could be seen that their decks were swarming with soldiers, and from the flagstaff of each waved the Stars and Strips. And there were hundreds in that crowd who saluted the flag with cheer after cheer, and from many a house a starry flag which had been concealed was brought out and flung to the breeze.

There was no resistance, and the soldiers landed as quietly as if there had been no war. The Southern men who had not fled, prudently kept quiet. The flag of the Union was raised over the capitol and there it floated never to come down.

Lawrence and Guilford lost no time in reporting to General Lyon. The General listened to what Guilford had to say, complimented him highly on what he had done, saying that he would see that he was properly rewarded.

With General Lyon to think was to act. Leaving a few hundred men to garrison Jefferson City, he at once made preparations to ascend the river to

Boonville. If the nation had had a dozen generals like Lyon the war would not have lasted a year.

When Lawrence and his party went to get their horses, Guilford told Lawrence he was not going with them. Instead, he said, he was going to Boonville by land, report to Governor Jackson, stay until he saw Lyon knock tar out of Marmaduke, and then go to Lexington. "And, Lawrence, I want you to swap horses with me, mine is tired." Lawrence did so, and shook hands with him thinking it might be for the last time. As for Guilford he rode away perfectly unconcerned. "Ta, ta," he said to Lawrence. "Tell General Lyon I will beat him to Boonville." And he did.

Lyon took possession of Jefferson City on the fifteenth of June, only four days after his meeting with Jackson and Price in St. Louis. Is it any wonder that his celerity astonished and disconcerted his enemies? On the sixteenth he was on his way up the river to Boonville with a force of scarcely seventeen hundred men. Until Guilford reported to him, he was under the impression he would have to fight at Boonville the forces of both Parsons and Marmaduke; but if Guilford was correct, he would have to fight Marmaduke only. Even if his foes had been twice as numerous, he would not have hesitated.

As for Guilford, he made good his boast; he rode into Boonville on the afternoon of the sixteenth, and reported to Governor Jackson. And in that report he showed his cunning. He reasoned that if he reported Lyon's force too large, Marmaduke would retire without a battle, therefore it was better to tell the truth. So he reported that Lyon was ascending the river with a force estimated at twelve hundred, having left the remainder of his force in Jefferson City, and in all probability he would be at Boonville during the coming night, or early the next day.

"So soon?" exclaimed the Governor, much perturbed.

"By to-morrow, at the farthest," replied Guilford.

"That Lyon is the very devil; he must have wings!" said the Governor. "Oh, that Parsons were here, but it will be impossible for Parsons to be here by to-morrow. Marmaduke, you must try and hold him off until Parsons comes."

"Governor, I can't do it, even if he has only twelve hundred men," replied Marmaduke. "My advice is to get out of here, and that quick."

"General, it will not do. If no more, you must hold him until I can remove our stores, and also give all citizens who wish to get away, an opportunity to do so. This will be bitter news to them, they expect us to hold the place."

"I will do all mortal man can," replied the General; "but prepare for the worst."

This conversation filled Guilford with delight.

He fairly chuckled as he pictured to himself Marmaduke's forces flying before the despised Yankees.

News now began to come in from other sources, that Lyon was on his way up the river. Meantime it began to be rumored through the city that it might have to be given up, and the excited populace thronged to Governor Jackson, and to General Marmaduke, to ask if it were so. They were told to hope for the best, but be prepared for the worst, and if they did not wish to fall into the hands of the Yankees, to be prepared to flee. And flee many of them did; they could imagine nothing worse than to fall in the hands of the dreaded Yankees, and Frank Blair's Dutch.

On the morning of the seventeenth, Lyon landed his troops, about eight miles below Boonville, and moved on the place by land. With a faint heart Marmaduke marched out to meet him. The forces first met about two miles out of the city, where, after a slight resistance, Marmaduke fell back to the edge of the city, where he made a more determined stand. But Lyon's men made a charge which swept everything before them; the State troops fled wildly through the city and out into the country, and the battle was over.

Such was the conflict which is known in history as the battle of Boonville; but in reality it was nothing but a skirmish, and a small one at that. Lyon had two men killed, and ten wounded. The loss of

Marmaduke was the same. But trifling as this engagement was, its results were grand. Afterwards great battles were fought, and thousands slain, where the results were not so far-reaching as were those of this battle of Boonville. In fact, it was a mighty victory for the Union.

Colonel Thomas L. Snead, General Price's Adjutant-general, in speaking of Boonville says:

"Insignificant as this engagement was, in a military aspect, it was in fact a stunning blow to the Southern Rights people of the State, and one which did an incalculable and unending injury to the Confederates. It was, indeed, the consummation of Blair's statesmanlike scheme to make it impossible for Missouri to secede. It was the crowning achievement of Lyon's well-conceived campaign. It made the Missouri River an unobstructed Federal highway from its source to its mouth, and made it impossible for Price to hold the State."

Guilford Craig witnessed the conflict, and when he saw the Confederates in disorganized retreat he could hardly refrain from shouting for joy. "Victory number one," he exclaimed to himself. "Now for Lexington and Price," and he joined in the disorderly retreat.

Small as the battle was, it made a profound impression on Lawrence. He had passed through tenfold greater danger in the riots which followed the capture of Camp Jackson, but never before had he seen hostile lines in battle array. The thunder of the cannon, the bursting shells, the hum of the Minié were all strange music to him. He bore himself well, and General Lyon complimented him on his coolness. The victory gave Lyon's troops unbounded confidence in their general, and they were ready and eager to follow him anywhere he might lead.

CHAPTER XXII

THE RACE TO SAVE SIGEL

A T Lexington, General Price found several thousand Confederates who had rushed there in obedience to the call of Governor Jackson; but they were unorganized, and many of them were without arms. Hardly had he begun to bring something like order out of the chaotic mass, when Guilford Craig came riding into camp bringing the news of the capture of Boonville, also despatches from Governor Jackson saying he was in full flight for the southern part of the State, and requesting the General to meet him there.

General Price saw that Lexington must be given up. Placing all the troops in Lexington and vicinity in command of General Rains, with orders to move south and join Governor Jackson at Warsaw, he took a small escort and started on a ride of nearly three hundred miles to northwest Arkansas to ask General McCulloch, who had gathered an army there, to come to the aid of Missouri, and help to redeem the State.

Before starting for the south, General Price warmly thanked Guilford Craig for his diligence, and left him behind to watch the movements of

Lyon, and to report to General Rains or Governor Jackson.

In a few days after the capture of Boonville, a young man was sent in from one of the outposts, with the information that he had presented himself to the guard, and asked to be conducted to Lieutenant Middleton. Lawrence saw it was Guilford Craig in his disguise, and lost no time in conducting him to General Lyon.

It was news, and important news, to Lyon that General Price had left the command of his army to General Rains, and had himself gone to Arkansas, leaving orders for Rains to evacuate Lexington and join the Governor at Warsaw. Lyon saw how important it was that he should strike the forces under Rains and the Governor, before they could get out of the State. At the beginning of the campaign, Lyon saw that if he drove Price from the Missouri River, he would retreat south, and for that reason had divided his forces, sending half of them into southwest Missouri under Sigel. The column under Sigel left St. Louis the same day that Lyon left by boat for Jefferson City. Sigel went by railroad as far as Rolla, one hundred and twenty-five miles. From there he made a rapid march of one hundred and twenty-five miles to Springfield. Leaving part of his force there, he pushed on to Neosho, eighty miles farther, with the remainder, about one thousand. This placed Sigel over two hundred miles from his base of supplies at Rolla, and directly in the path over which Governor Jackson would have to retreat.

Hearing that Jackson was approaching Carthage, Sigel left about one hundred men at Neosho, and marched north with the rest of his force to meet Jackson. Why Sigel left these few men at Neosho is past finding out. He had not been gone more than twenty-four hours, before this single company was attacked by at least a thousand men, and forced to surrender. By this foolish move, Sigel lost a tenth of his little army; and with less than a thousand men he met Jackson nine miles north of Carthage. Jackson had, at least, five thousand men. The fight was too unequal; Sigel was forced to retreat, and the Federals were driven back through Carthage. Sigel was now in a precarious situation. Before him was Governor Jackson with an army of thousands, in his rear were Generals Price and McCulloch with an army five times as numerous as his own; and now commenced his famous retreat to Springfield, nearly one hundred miles away. He kept his little army intact, beat back every attack of the enemy, and arrived in Springfield in safety.

General Lyon at Boonville knew full well the value of time, and that to be successful he must follow closely on the heels of Governor Jackson in his retreat south. But try as hard as he might, it was the third of July before he could get transportation

Guilford Craig came riding into camp, bringing despatches

and supplies to move, and Jackson was a full week ahead of him. He left Boonville with a force of a little over two thousand. At Clinton he was joined by Major Sturgis with a force of twenty-five hundred, giving him an army of forty-five hundred.

During the stop at Boonville, Lawrence organized a splendid scouting force. Most of them had seen service on the plains, and nearly one-half had figured in the Kansas troubles. Take them together they were a bold, reckless set, and could be depended on in any emergency.

On the second day's march from Boonville, Lawrence asked permission to take a dozen of his best scouts and try to locate Jackson's army, going as far as Springfield, if need be. With a dozen of his scouts, Lawrence thought he would be able to beat off any roving band of the enemy he might fall in with.

General Lyon gave him permission, and Lawrence chose a dozen of his best men. At that time, the blue had not been adopted by all Federal soldiers, as the color of their uniform. The color of the uniform of the First Iowa was gray, and Lawrence chose that color for his scouts, so that if need be they could easily pass themselves off for Confederate soldiers. The first day out the party met with no adventures of any moment. They fell in with a few small parties of Confederates who claimed they, too, were seeking to join Jackson, but whom Lawrence suspected of being nothing more than bands of guerillas.

On the second day, they overtook a company of nearly thirty men, who on discovering them, fired a scattering volley, and took to the woods. Lawrence and his party charged, and succeeded in capturing half a dozen of them. Upon questioning his prisoners, Lawrence learned that instead of being Confederates, they were a company of Home Guards, on their way to Springfield to join a regiment which was being raised there. They had taken the scouts for Confederates, and firing one volley had scattered like sheep. Lawrence dryly remarked that if all Home Guards were as valiant as they, the Confederates had little to fear. The Guards hung their heads, but excused themselves by saying they were poorly armed, and that they had no idea how many there were in the supposed party of Confederates. Lawrence learned from them that Jackson and his army had passed some miles west and were now well on their way southwards. But all had the same story to tell, of the atrocities being inflicted on the Union men. No man's life was safe who was suspected of Union sentiments.

Leaving this party to make its way to Springfield the best it could, Lawrence rode on somewhat disturbed over what he had heard. If Jackson was as far ahead of Lyon as the Home Guards had reported, and had half as many men, Sigel might be having trouble. Therefore Lawrence pressed on with renewed haste. Along in the afternoon they came to a hamlet, and soon saw that something unusual was going on. A party of at least twenty rough-looking men were gathered around an individual who seemed to be held a prisoner, and now and then Lawrence thought he heard an agonized cry of a woman. But he did not have long to wait to know what it meant, for no sooner was the approach of the scouts discovered, than two of the men rode forward to meet them.

"Halt!" cried one of the men. "One of you'ns ride for'ard, an' tell we'uns who you'ns air."

Lawrence told his men to be prepared for any emergency, and then rode forward alone to meet the men. He noticed that the crowd of men with the exception of two who remained guarding the prisoner, had scattered to their horses, which were hitched to a rude railing in front of a dilapidated-looking store.

"We may have some trouble," thought Lawrence, but he rode forward as if perfectly unconcerned.

"Well, what do you want, and why did you halt us?" he asked.

"We'uns want to know who you'ns air, an' that quick," replied the man, with an oath.

"What if I decline to tell?" asked Lawrence.

The man tapped the butt of his revolver. "It will be the wors' for you'ns," he growled.

"That is a game two can play at," laughed Lawrence, "but whom do you take us for?"

"Don't know. You'ns air dressed like Confeds, but you'ns look like damn Yanks."

"Are you Confed or Yank?"

"Don't insult us, stranger, by calling us Yanks."

"That is all right, don't think we will fight. We are from St. Louis, and are on our way to Jackson's army," replied Lawrence. "Glad to meet you, but what is the excitement ahead?"

"We'uns have jest caught a Lincolnite, and we'uns air goin' to hang him."

"Good! can't you let us in to see the fun?"

"Sure," and he turned around and waved to the crowd, that it was all right.

Lawrence rode back to his scouts, and in a few words told them what was up. "And, boys," he added, "we must rescue that man. Pretend you are greatly interested in the affair, and to get a good view ride around until we have them surrounded. There are not over twenty of them. We can handle them. Shoot the first one who shows resistance. Now come on."

It was a pathetic scene which met the sight of the scouts. Under a tree with a rope around his neck, stood a large rough-looking man, with his hands bound behind him. There was no fear in his face, but he stood sullen and defiant like a wild beast at bay. At the feet of the one who seemed to be the leader of the mob knelt a woman, and a girl about twelve years of age, while with uplifted hands, and the tears running down their cheeks, they were praying for the life of the husband and father. The man answered their appeals with curses, and shouted, "Take an' string him up, boys, we'uns have had enough of this snivellin'." The prisoner was roughly seized and jerked under an overhanging limb, but the wife sprang to her feet, and with a cry of agony, threw her arms around her husband, clinging to him with desperation. It took two strong men to unclasp her grasp, and then they flung her backwards with such force that she fell and lay stunned on the ground.

The effect on the prisoner was terrible. His face flamed with the passions of a demon. With a mighty effort he wrenched himself loose from those who held him, and springing forward, planted a kick in the stomach of one of the ruffians which doubled him up like a jack-knife, and he lay still and white on the ground.

"Look! See! He has killed Jake," shouted the leader. "Seize him! String him up! Hold the woman; make her look at him while he kicks the air."

Half a dozen men sprang forward to do the bidding of their leader. The prisoner's hands being bound, he could do little to resist.

This diversion gave Lawrence the opportunity he was looking for. All the Confederates had left their horses and were crowding around their victim. At a sign from Lawrence the scouts, as if seeking a point of advantage to see the execution, surrounded the gang.

"Swing him up," shouted the leader, as the rope around the man's neck was thrown over a projecting limb. Half a dozen strong hands seized the rope.

"Hold!" cried Lawrence in a voice of thunder. "Hands up, every one."

The would-be murderers looked up in amazement. Around them on their horses sat twelve men, in the hand of each a cocked revolver.

"Hands up!" again commanded Lawrence. "Boys, shoot the first one who reaches for a weapon."

The leader of the gang failed to obey. The revolver in the hand of Dan Sherman cracked, and the leader fell dead with a ball through the brain. The rest of the party put their hands up in a hurry.

"Thunderation! Yanks after all," muttered the fellow who had ridden out to meet Lawrence. "I might have knowed it."

As for the prisoner and his wife and daughter, they stood for a time as if rooted to the ground. The wife was the first to comprehend what had happened. With a wild cry of joy, she threw her arms around her husband, and sobbed. "Saved! Saved!"

"Line up here," commanded Lawrence of his prisoners, and they formed in line. There were nineteen of them. The one who had been kicked had recovered consciousness, but lay on the ground moaning. "Boys, keep them covered," said Lawrence, "while I see to the man they were to hang; and you, Dan, see to their arms."

The cords which bound the wrists of the man were cut, and the rope was removed from around his neck, but he still stood as in a daze. The bitterness and fear of death had been his, and he could not realize that the grim monster had been cheated of his prey. But the wife did, and she nearly smothered Lawrence with her embraces. "God only can reward you," she exclaimed, her tears falling like rain. Then turning to her husband, she cried, "Jim, Jim, why don't you'ns thank this gentleman? Thank them all!"

The man brushed his hand before his eyes, as if sweeping away a mist, and then felt of his neck.

"That rope," he exclaimed, "that rope, it burned like fire."

"It will trouble you no more," said Lawrence. "It gives me pleasure to present you alive and well to your wife and daughter."

The man now began to comprehend he was saved,

and was in his way as profuse in his thanks as his wife and child had been.

In the meantime Dan Sherman had been removing the arms of the prisoners, and a goodly assortment he had when through. How to dispose of the arms was the next question. A well was discovered, and into this the arms were thrown, and several large rocks rolled in on top of them. "I reckon," said Dan, " them rocks will hold them down."

The man who had come so near to being hanged now told his story. His name was James Ferguson. Several of his Union neighbors had been driven from their homes, but he had resolved to stick. Being known as a man of courage, for some time he was let alone, but the previous day he was waylaid, and in beating off his assailants, killed one of them. He then knew that his only safety lay in flight, but his foes surprised him as he was saddling his horse,

"That," said he, "was last night. They burned my cabin, drove off my stock, and left my wife an' little gal with only the clothes they had on. They followed me here, as you see."

"And what will you do now?" asked Lawrence.

"Go with you'ns if you'ns will let me."

"But your wife and daughter, what of them?"

"Let them go too, as far as Springfield. I will see them safe, and then go in the army."

"Can your wife and daughter ride?" asked Lawrence.

"Ride, stranger," replied the man, "they will ride as hard and as far as any of you'ns."

"Then," said Lawrence, "pick out three of the best horses hitched here, and come along."

The question now arose what to do with the prisoners. It was impossible to take them along, so they were paroled and let go.

"I ought to hang every blessed one of you," said Lawrence, "and if I hear of any more of your deviltry, I will come back and do it."

Their surly and revengeful looks showed they would be good until their captors got out of sight, and no longer.

More than an hour had been lost by the scouts, and they now rode rapidly forward. Some five or six miles had been passed, when a lone horseman appeared in front riding rapidly toward them. When he noticed the scouts, he drew rein and carefully scrutinized them, then came leisurely on. When he drew near Lawrence saw to his amazement that it was Guilford Craig. The horse he was on was white with foam, and showed it had been ridden hard. Lawrence was about to speak his name, when a sign from Guilford showed that he did not wish to be known, so Lawrence spoke to him as a stranger.

"Where now, my friend? You seem to be in a hurry," said Lawrence.

"I am," was the answer, "please let me pass in peace."

"Sorry, but I will have to interview you first," replied Lawrence.

"Then let me speak to you in private," answered Guilford.

They rode to one side, and then Guilford told Lawrence that the forces of Governor Jackson had met Sigel near Carthage, defeated him, and that Sigel was in the greatest danger of losing his entire force.

The news astonished Lawrence. Sigel defeated, and Lyon miles away! Lawrence groaned as he thought of what might be the consequences.

"I am carrying despatches back for Governor Jackson," continued Guilford, "to prominent secessionists at Lexington and Boonville. But I must first find Lyon, and let him read the despatches."

Lawrence was at first puzzled as to what he had best do, ride on and find out the fate of Sigel, or escort Guilford back to Lyon, ostensibly a prisoner.

"Go on, by all means," said Guilford, "you may be of some help to Sigel. Do not fear for me. I shall be much safer, and make better time alone."

Lawrence thought so, but told him what had happened a few miles back, and said that some of the crowd might be at the hamlet and make him trouble.

"I do not fear them," replied Guilford, "I have papers from Governor Jackson that will pass me anywhere where his name is honored."

"All right," said Lawrence, "I will go on, but for the love of Heaven, get to Lyon as quick as you can."

"That I will, and you get to Sigel. Good-bye."

"It is all right, boys, let him pass," said Lawrence.

Dan Sherman took a chew of tobacco, and looking after Guilford, said: "If that young fellow had a mustache and curly hair, I would swear it was Charley Morris, the one who put the joke up on Colonel Bell. Say, Lieutenant, what became of Morris? He was as sharp as lightning."

"Oh, Lyon kept him," answered Lawrence. "But, boys, that fellow told me some bad news."

"What's that?" they all asked.

"That the forces under Governor Jackson met Sigel near Carthage, defeated him, and that Sigel's entire force is in danger of capture."

"The devil," was the profane reply. "What are you going to do now, Lieutenant?"

"Ride on and do what we can to help Sigel."

"Hurrah!" they shouted. "We are with you, Lieutenant. We are good for any hundred of Jackson's ragamuffins," and they rode on, eager for what was ahead.

When Guilford Craig was out of sight and hearing of Lawrence and his party, he halted, dismounted, hung his hat on a bush, stepped back a few feet, and fired a ball through the crown. He looked at the hole critically, and said: "All right. No burnt-powder stains there," and remounting, rode on. When he reached the hamlet where Lawrence had rescued Ferguson, he found that the crowd instead of diminishing had been augmented. The man that Ferguson had kicked was said to be dying, and the greatest excitement prevailed. Terrible imprecations were being heaped upon the heads of the Yankees, and so high did the feeling run, that the one who had ridden out to meet Lawrence and reported the party all right was threatened with the same fate which they had intended to mete out to Ferguson.

No sooner did Guilford Craig appear, than he was surrounded. Who was he? Where did he come from? Where was he going? Did he meet a party of Yanks?

"One question at a time, gentlemen," said Guilford. "I am a messenger from Governor Jackson bearing good news. He met the Dutch General, Sigel, at Carthage the other day and whipped him blind."

"Hurrah!" shouted the crowd, "but did you meet any Yankees?"

"Yes, about an hour or two ago. Took them for our fellows at first, and they nearly got me. Escaped by jumping my horse over a fence. Look here," and he took off his hat, and showed them.

"Close call that," said one, "but not as close as poor Duncan got. They took him plumb between the eyes." And then Guilford had to listen to the story of the rescue of Ferguson.

"Blame cute trick," said Guilford. "You will have to look sharp when Yankees are around. Wonder what those fellows could be doing. Lyon can't be far off."

"What! Lyon coming this way!" they shouted.

"Yes, and if he does, you fellows had better look a little out. But I must be going. Say, don't some of you fellows want to swap horses with me? My horse is a good one, but he is tired out. Jackson told me to kill half a dozen horses if I wanted to, but get to Lexington."

A horse trade appealed to them, and one fellow looking over Guilford's horse carefully, reckoned he would trade. "My hoss is n't as good a looker as you'ns," he remarked, "but he is a goer."

Guilford traded and found that the horse was a vicious brute, but as tough as a knot, and that was what he wanted. He rode on through the remainder of the day and through the night, taking no rest until he reached the outposts of Lyon near Osceola. Between him and Lyon lay the swollen Osage River. Leaving his horse, he assumed his disguise, whereupon Guilford Craig disappeared, and Charles Morris appeared on the scene.

Securing a skiff, he crossed the river, and was

soon closeted with the General. Lyon was astounded at the news of Sigel's defeat. He now saw that all hopes of capturing Jackson and his army had vanished. It must have been a crushing blow to him, but he made no complaint, found no fault. He only said, " I must save Sigel! I must save Sigel!"

He then read the despatches which Guilford had brought from Governor Jackson. His brow clouded as he read, for the despatches showed that some who stood high up, and posed as Union men, were in reality traitors. He read all the despatches carefully, took notes, then resealing them, handed them back to Guilford.

" Deliver them as Jackson ordered," he said. "You must do nothing to arouse suspicion. Now that I know what is in them, they can do little harm."

The next day Charles Morris had disappeared, and Guilford Craig was on his way to Lexington as a Confederate messenger. As for Lyon, his one desire was to save Sigel. He had to cross the swollen Osage River by ferry, and it took him a whole day to do it. But by the morning of July 11, his whole force was across, and he started for Springfield, eighty miles away.

All through that hot July day, they marched. The burning sun beat down upon them, but there was no stop, no stay. Evening came, and they halted. A hurried cup of coffee was made, the bacon broiled on the end of a stick,—this and hard crackers was their meal. Then on through the night they marched, and when morning came, they were fifty miles from where they started. Fifty miles in twenty-four hours did those boys fresh from the fields of Kansas, Iowa, and Missouri march under the burning sun and through the darkness of the night, that Sigel might be saved. It was a feat hardly ever equalled in military annals. Oh, that the Union had had more Generals like Lyon, more soldiers like those who marched with him!

They were now within thirty miles of Springfield. But here they were met by Lawrence who had hastened back, bringing the word that Sigel was safe. The army now moved more slowly and by the thirteenth was in Springfield. But Price and Jackson had escaped, and along the Arkansas border a mighty army was gathering to crush Lyon; and a great nation was doing nothing to help.

CHAPTER XXIII

WILSON CREEK

THE entire force which Lyon could muster at Springfield did not much exceed six thousand, and of these not over five thousand were effective. Gathering to oppose him was an army variously estimated at from fifteen to twenty thousand. Lyon saw that he would have to be reinforced, if he held Springfield. To give it up would be to relinquish the whole of southwest Missouri to the enemy, therefore he made an urgent appeal for reinforcements.

A change had taken place in the Commander of the Department of the West. Instead of appointing General Lyon, as was his due, the War Department appointed General John C. Frémont. Frémont had been the Republican nominee for President in 1856, and was the idol of the radical wing of the Republican party. The appointment was more political than military, but Frémont's friends predicted great things of him, and looked upon him as the coming general.

After receiving the appointment, Frémont lingered for some days in New York, and to Lyon's appeals for reinforcements gave little heed. He did not come to St. Louis until he was peremptorily ordered to do so by General Scott. He reached St. Louis on the twenty-fifth of July and found a task before him which he little understood, and which called for the highest military genius. The disloyal sentiment which he found in St. Louis appalled him. Fearing for his own safety, he proceeded to protect himself by organizing a bodyguard of one hundred men. It was composed of stalwart men mounted on powerful horses, and their uniforms were gorgeous to behold, equal to a troop of drum-majors. But they were brave men, all the same, and afterwards won imperishable honor by their charge at Springfield.

Frémont now promised to send Lyon five thousand men. Had he done so history would have read differently, but he failed to keep his promise. There were soldiers in St. Louis who could have been spared. There were no Confederate troops of any great number within hundreds of miles of the place, but Frémont conceived the idea that the city was in danger, and planned an expedition down the Mississippi. Lyon was left to his fate; his appeal for reinforcement unheeded.

For Lyon to give up what he had won would be to give Missouri back to Jackson and Price; he could not do it; he would stay and fight, if need be he would die.

When Frémont heard that Lyon would stay and fight, he coolly remarked: "If he fights he will do it upon his own responsibility."

Oh, the injustice of it! Never was so heroic a general left so coolly to his fate.

After the defeat of Sigel at Carthage, Price and McCulloch joined forces, and made preparations to advance on Springfield. Their forces were being continually augmented by recruits from Missouri and Arkansas, while Lyon's army from sickness and hardships was growing weaker. The Confederate generals knew these facts, and expected an easy victory.

It was a busy time with Lawrence and his scouts while Lyon lay at Springfield. There was hardly a day but they came in collision with scouts from Price's army, and from their daring and marksmanship, they came more to be feared than a regiment of cavalry. So closely did they guard Springfield, that General Price complained that even his scouts and spies could bring him no information as to the movements of Lyon. "I cannot even find out," he exclaimed, "whether he has fortified Springfield or not."

Even Guilford Craig, who had returned from his northern trip, and of whom General Price hoped great things, reported that he had been unable to get into Springfield. But Guilford did not want to get into Springfield. If he had, he would have been obliged to make some kind of a report. But he had met Lawrence more than once, and through him was enabled to inform Lyon of every movement of the Confederates. He reported that the combined strength of the Confederates was about twenty thousand, but that not more than twelve or fifteen thousand were effective, and that McCulloch and Price were quarrelling as to who should have supreme command.

The last of July Lawrence reported that the Confederates had begun their forward movement, and were advancing in three different columns. Lyon resolved to march out and strike the columns in detail. His advance struck the brigade of General Rains at Dug Springs, some twenty-two miles out of Springfield. It was not a fight, but a foot race, Rains's men fleeing in the wildest confusion. The Confederates took the alarm, and rapidly concentrated their forces. Lyon, not wishing to fight a general battle so far from Springfield, returned. The enemy now slowly advanced, until within ten miles of Springfield. Lyon now concluded to stake all on a battle.

During these trying days, Lawrence saw that the nervous strain was telling on his beloved commander; he was growing thinner, and slept little. He had now given up all hopes of receiving reinforcement. He now must fight or retreat, and he resolved to fight. Lawrence always thought that Lyon felt that he was going to his death, that the country he had served so faithfully had deserted him in his hour of extremity. But he uttered no complaint.

Death to him was sweeter than flight. He knew that if he retreated, all Missouri would be lost with the exception of St. Louis. It was better for him to die, that the State might be saved.

On the ninth of August, during a scout, Lawrence met a small party of Confederates and put them to flight. One of them lingered a little longer than the rest, before he wheeled his horse to retreat, and as if by accident, he dropped a paper. Lawrence was almost sure it was Guilford Craig. He secured the paper — it was but a scrap — and read: " I dare not meet you. You will be attacked to-morrow." It was not much, but it was enough. Swiftly Lawrence rode back to Lyon with the news. The General smiled grimly, and said: " I will save them the trouble, I will do the attacking."

Lyon's plans were well arranged. He was to give battle with the main body of his troops, while Sigel with twelve hundred men was to make a detour, and fall upon the flank and rear of the enemy.

The Confederates had no idea that Lyon would advance to meet them, and that night slept in fancied security. But at sunrise the next morning Lyon was on them. Sigel's movement at first was a perfect success. He struck their camp in the rear of the Confederate army at dawn, driving the surprised inmates out in the wildest confusion. Discipline seemed now to be at an end in Sigel's command. Many of his men left the ranks to plunder the captured camps. He saw the enemy forming to attack him, and made preparations to meet them. A gray-coated regiment burst out of the thicket in his front.

"Don't fire! don't fire!" was the cry, "it is the First Iowa!"

In a moment, the Third Louisiana, for it was that regiment, was upon them, firing into their faces. The effect was indescribable. A panic seized Sigel's men; all discipline was lost. There was no effort made to rally the men. The Texas cavalry followed them cutting them down as they fled. Sigel himself reached Springfield before the battle ended, accompanied by only one orderly. Although his men had to retreat directly behind Lyon's force, not a man of them came to help him. Lyon had to fight the battle alone, and there with three thousand, five hundred men, on Bloody Hill he put up such a battle as was never before fought on this continent. There amid the tangled thickets was fought a battle, by raw troops, on both sides, that the veterans of Napoleon never excelled. It was a battle which tells in letters of living light of the valor of the American soldier.

Where the battle raged the fiercest, there was Lyon cheering on his men. Again and again did the Confederates' thousands hurl themselves against his thin lines, only to be flung back bleeding and torn. Amid the thick underbrush the opposing forces were often only a few yards apart, and they poured their fire almost into each other's faces. In the darkened woods there were death grapples and deeds of valor of which the world never heard. Sometimes the lines would swing apart, and the thickets would hide the combatants from each other, and the field would become strangely silent. These periods of silence were harder to bear than the roar of the conflict. Then suddenly the thickets would again burst into flame and smoke, and the struggle would be renewed.

During these hours of carnage, Lawrence was everywhere in the thickest of the fray, carrying the orders of his beloved chieftain, cheering on the wavering, turning back the skulker. Already he had had two horses shot under him. He had just reported that Plummer had been driven back, when large masses of the enemy burst out of the thicket, and came on a charge. The only troops available to oppose them were the First Iowa.

"Come on, boys! I will lead you," shouted Lyon, and dashing to the front, he took off his hat, and swinging it over his head, cheered them on. Close by his side rode Lawrence. With a mighty shout the regiment sprang forward, and the enemy recoiled before them; but Lawrence saw the General reel in his saddle, and sprang from his horse just in time to receive him in his arms as he fell. Gently he laid him down, but the brave spirit had already fled — General Lyon had been shot through the heart. The tears gushed from Lawrence's eyes, as he gazed into the face now so peaceful in death.

Just then Carl Mayer came along, his right arm broken. He reported every officer in his company killed or disabled, and nearly half of the regiment gone.* Mayor Schofield, Lyon's Chief of Staff, now rode up, and gazed on the dead face of his General with tear-dimmed eyes.

" I will go to the company," said Lawrence to Carl, " I can now do no good here."

The company received Lawrence with a cheer. " We 'll get 'em yet! " shouted a powder-begrimed youth, whom Lawrence recognized as a quiet school-boy he had known in St. Louis. But that schoolboy had in him the heart of a hero. The enemy were forming for their last desperate effort. On they came with that peculiar cheer, afterwards known as the "Rebel yell."

On, on they came until their breasts almost touched the muzzles of the First Missouri's guns. Then, they wavered, halted, their lines quivering like the giant branches of a tree in a storm.

" They break; they run! " shouted Lawrence, " Charge! "

Right on their line rode Lawrence. His horse fell dead. Springing to his feet, he drew his sword, and pressed on. In front of him was a young Con-

*The First Missouri lost three hundred in this battle; the First Kansas nearly as many; and the First Iowa one hundred and fifty-four.

federate officer imploring his men not to give way. A soldier who had fought his way to Lawrence's side, lunged at the officer with his bayonet. The officer beat down the gun with a blow of his sword, but the weapon broke at the hilt, and he stood defenceless. Again the soldier raised his gun to lunge. Lawrence to his horror saw that the young officer was none other than his cousin. With a cry he sprang forward, and beat down the gun with his sword, just as the bayonet touched Edward's breast.

At this moment a squad of Confederates had rallied, and were rushing to the relief of their officer. At their head was Benton Shelley. He recognized Lawrence, and a look of joy came over his face, as he shouted, " At last we have met, renegade," and, raising his revolver, fired. Lawrence pitched forward on his face, and a moment later, the brave soldier who had stood by his side, fell across him dead.

Seeing Lawrence fall, his men rushed forward, and the Confederates were driven back in disorder. All along the line the charge had been repulsed, and the enemy were driven from the hill, back into their camps.

The hill for which the Union forces had struggled for five long hours was theirs, but along its sides, and amid its tangled thickets more than two thousand soldiers, Federals and Confederates, lay dead and wounded. Well has it been called ever since

With a cry he sprang forward and beat down the gun with
his sword

"Bloody Hill." With the last repulse of the enemy, the noise of battle died away. The Federal officers held a hasty council, and it was decided that their safety consisted in falling back. It was true, they held the battlefield, but the enemy could surround them, and cut them off from Springfield. Therefore the army which had whipped three or four times their number, sullenly fell back. But the enemy did not follow, they had had enough of fighting.

During the night, another council was held by the Federal officers, and it was decided to retreat back to Rolla. In the morning the weary march of one hundred and twenty-five miles was began and on the whole retreat they were not molested. The enemy were satisfied with the possession of Springfield. But the shame of it! When the army retreated from Springfield, they left the body of their brave commander to be buried by the enemy.

Although the Federal army retreated from the battlefield, they had won; they had saved Missouri. The battle of Wilson Creek was the crowning glory of Lyon's life. It was, in effect, a great victory. Read what Colonel Stead, General Price's Adjutant-general, and afterwards Chief of Staff says:

"Lyon did not fight and die in vain. Through him the rebellion which Blair had organized, and to which he had himself given force and strength, had succeeded at last. By capturing the State Militia at Camp Jackson, and driving the Governor from the capital, and all his troops into the uttermost corner of the State, and by holding Price and McCulloch at bay, he had given the Union men of Missouri time, opportunity, and courage to bring their State Convention together again, and had given the Convention an excuse and the power to depose Governor Jackson and Lieutenant-governor Reynolds, to vacate the seats of the members of the General Assembly, and to establish a State Government which was loyal to the Union, and which would use the whole organized power of the State, its Treasury, its Credit, its Militia, and all its great resources to sustain the Union and crush the South. All this had been done while Lyon was boldly confronting the overwhelming strength of Price and McCulloch. Had he abandoned Springfield instead, and opened to Price a pathway to the Missouri; had he not been willing to die for the freedom of the negro and for the preservation of the Union, none of these things would have been done. By wisely planning, by boldly doing, and by bravely dying, *he had won the fight for Missouri.*"

CHAPTER XXIV

AFTER THE BATTLE

WHEN Lawrence came to himself, he was in an ambulance, jolting over the rough roads, on his way to Rolla. The ball from the revolver of Benton Shelley had struck him on the left side of the head, ploughing along the skull, not fracturing it, but producing concussion of the brain. After the repulse of the enemy, he was found by his comrades, and they, seeing that there was still life in him, carried him back and placed him in an ambulance. He was well on his way toward Rolla before he recovered consciousness, and then it was to learn that the army was retreating, and that the body of his General had been left to the tender mercy of his foes.

This greatly excited him: "Cowards! cowards!" he exclaimed. "Oh! why did I leave him? Why did they not leave me, and a score of others like me, and bring along his precious remains?"

By the time Lawrence reached Rolla he had a raging fever, was delirious, and recked nothing of what was going on around him. When next consciousness came to his bewildered brain, a sweet-faced nurse was sitting by his side. It seemed to him he was surrounded with familiar objects, yet so weak was he, to raise even his eyelids was such an effort, that he took little heed. The nurse noticed that he stirred, and when she looked, and saw the light of reason in his eyes, she murmured, " Thank God."

He tried to speak, but could only faintly whisper.

" There, there!" said the nurse as gently as if hushing a child, " Don't try to talk; you have been very sick, but you will be better now. Here, take this," and she placed a soothing draught to his lips. He took it, sighed, closed his eyes, and sank into a refreshing sleep.

When he awoke, it was night, the room was dimly lighted, and the same sweet-faced nurse was sitting at a table reading. He tried to speak, but he was so weak, so weak; yet he felt no pain. The nurse heard him and hurried to his side. " Ah! you are better," she said smiling. " There! no talking, no questions. You will know all, when you are able to hear. Now you are to take this, it will give you strength."

She gave him broth which he eagerly swallowed, and then he closed his eyes, and slept once more. When he awoke again it was day, and there was no one in the room. He looked around. Was he dreaming? Surely this was his old room at his uncle's, the same furniture, the same pictures on the walls. But in addition to the pictures, there was a sword hanging on the wall above his head. He knew it well, it was his sword, the "Sword of Bunker Hill." What did it mean? The last thing that he remembered was being in an ambulance, on that fearful journey back to Rolla.

The nurse came in, and who was with her but Doctor Goodnow? Lawrence knew him in an instant. He was as fat and as jolly as ever. Lawrence grew more bewildered. Was what he was seeing an illusion? But there was no illusion in the merry voice of the Doctor, as he exclaimed : " Awake, are you, you young scamp? You came near slipping through my fingers; but you will live, another monument to the great skill of Yours Truly. But I ought to have let you die, you pesky Yank."

" Doctor! Doctor!" cried Lawrence weakly, " Where am I? And how did you come here? "

" Where are you? " answered the Doctor. " Thank your stars you are in your uncle's house in St. Louis, you young reprobate. And how did I come here? Well, ask some of Abe Lincoln's hirelings. We have been having lively times up in old Platte. John Brown and the Kansas troubles nothing to it! We are all Rebels in Platte. A regiment of Iowa soldiers swooped down on us, and, blast their eyes, if they didn't want me to take an oath of allegiance to Abe Lincoln's government! Did I do it? Not much, so they shipped me down here. They let me go, after a while. Your uncle told me about you, and, hope to be shot, if I did n't work like a Trojan to save your life. Ought to be hanged for doing it."

Lawrence could not help smiling at what the Doctor said. " And Judge Lindsly, what of him? " he asked.

" Arrested too. Think of the old Judge taking such an oath! He would die ten thousand times first. But they have let him go now. You have talked enough, not another word."

" Can't I see uncle and aunt? "

" No, not now. Can't be responsible for sending you to Hades before your time. That place is filling up with Yankees fast enough. Take some broth, go to sleep, and when you get strong enough you can see your uncle and aunt. I am commander, and mind you obey me."

It was a couple of days before the Doctor would allow Lawrence to see his uncle and aunt, because he knew the interview would be a trying one. When they did come in, his aunt pressed kiss after kiss on his pale cheeks, and her tears fell like rain, as she murmured: " My dear, dear Lawrence, how can I ever be grateful enough for what you have done? "

" Done? " answered Lawrence in surprise. " Why, aunt, for what I have done I thought I had nearly broken your heart. Have I not fought against those you love? Am I not an enemy to the South you hold so dear? "

"Oh, Lawrence, I forgive you all that; it is for saving the life of my boy, my darling Edward, that I thank you."

"How in the world did you know I saved the life of Edward?" asked Lawrence.

"We have received a letter from him," she replied, "telling us all about that dreadful battle, and how you saved his life, and he feared lost your own. Guilford—I—I mean a messenger from the Confederate army brought the letters."

Her confusion was so great, that Lawrence said: "Do not be alarmed, dear aunt, if Guilford Craig did bring the letters. Not for the world would I betray him, even if he were ten times the spy that he is."

Little did Mrs. Middleton think that every one of those letters had been opened, their contents noted, and the edges carefully resealed, before being delivered.

"Thank you, Lawrence," said his aunt, "it is no more than I might expect of you. But let me read that part of Edward's letter which refers to you."

"Better let me thank him first," said his uncle, "Clara, you are doing all the talking."

It was a warm grasp of the hand that his uncle gave him. "My boy," he exclaimed, "remember that after this, my home is your home, I don't care how much of a Yankee you become."

Lawrence was deeply touched by these expressions of gratitude, and his eyes filled with tears.

" Now," said his aunt gayly, " for the letter," and she read:

"Of course you have heard before this of the dreadful battle we fought near Springfield. Thank God, we were victorious in the end, and now we hold Springfield, but at a terrible cost. Hundreds of our best and bravest men fell, and, dear father and mother, you would have no son now, if my life had not been saved by Lawrence; and I fear, in exchange, he gave his own. A huge soldier lunged at me with his bayonet; I beat down his gun with my sword, but it broke at the hilt, with the force of the blow, and I was left defenceless. The soldier lunged at me again, and just as the bayonet reached my breast, I heard a voice cry, 'Not him! not him!' and swift as a lightning stroke there came a mighty blow, and the bayonet was beaten down. So close was the point of the bayonet to me, it tore my clothes in its downward course. It was Lawrence who struck the blow and saved my life. Now comes the saddest part of the story. Seeing me almost surrounded by the enemy, Benton Shelley led a party to my rescue. Seeing Lawrence, he raised his revolver and fired, when but a few feet from him. Lawrence fell headlong, and in a moment more, the soldier who attempted my life fell dead across him.

We were now charged, and forced back. I cannot blame Benton, but I do feel hard toward him for boasting of what he did. You know Benton disliked Lawrence, and swore that if they ever met on the battlefield one or the other would die. Somehow I can never feel toward Benton as I did. After the battle, I searched for the body of Lawrence among the slain, but could not find it, and a faint hope arose that he might have been only wounded. Let father spare no pains in finding out whether he was brought back with the wounded or not, and if he was, take and care for him for my sake. Ask him to forgive what I have done and said against him."

"That is all," said his aunt, wiping her eyes. "And now, Lawrence, you understand why you are here. Your uncle went to Rolla, and after a long search found you, delirious, and near unto death. He had little trouble in getting permission to bring you home. They thought you would die any way. I do not know but you would have died, if good Doctor Goodnow had not appeared about that time. That queer man will sit and curse the Yankees by the hour, and yet he has watched over you like a father."

"I owe much to Doctor Goodnow," said Lawrence. "I shall always remember him."

"Do you see that sword?" said his uncle, pointing to the sword which hung over the head of

Lawrence's bed. "They tell me it was found grasped in your hand when you were picked up unconscious on the field."

"Yes," replied Lawrence, "it is the sword you gave me,— the 'Sword of Bunker Hill.' It is the sword which struck down the bayonet reaching for Edward's heart. Thank God it saved life, instead of taking it!"

"Amen," replied his uncle devoutly.

Two or three days afterwards Doctor Goodnow came in to bid Lawrence good-bye. "I am off," he said.

"Off where, to Platte County?" asked Lawrence.

"No, to Price's army. The boys need me. You will not give me away, will you?"

"Not I, Doc," replied Lawrence. "The best thing I can ask is that if any poor sick or wounded Yanks should fall into Price's hands, you will be there to attend them."

"Cuss the Yankees! I will poison them, so I will."

But after all that the Doctor had said, there was a queer quiver in his voice, as he bade Lawrence good-bye for the last time.

And here we will leave Lawrence, surrounded and cared for by those who loved him, although enemies of the flag for which he fought. When well, he again took part in the great struggle then going on, but on other fields, and under other commanders.

THE END

275
70
193,50
220
194,70

(D) 708
70
8
10